The Retreat Handbook

The Retreat Handbook

Sandy and Larry Reimer

MOREHOUSE-BARLOW
Wilton, CT

Morehouse-Barlow Co., Inc.
78 Danbury Road
Wilton, Connecticut 06897

ISBN 0-8192-1393-4

Library of Congress Catalog Card Number

Printed in the United States of America

10 9 8 7 6 5 4 3 2 1

2 4 6 8 10 9 7 5 3 1

To our parents,
who always encouraged and supported our retreats
ALVIN AND EVELYN SEBASTIAN
JOHN AND ALBERTA REIMER.

Contents

Section IV: The Planning Retreat

Appendix

Acknowledgments

This book is a compilation of experiences and learnings which we have integrated during our years of ministry. We thank the churches and the people who offered retreats for us when we were in high school: St. Luke Lutheran Church in Silver Spring, Maryland and First Congregational Church in River Edge, New Jersey and particularly Kermit Finstad and Marie Brown. We appreciate the churches and conferences where we led our first retreats: First Congregational Church in North Branford, Connecticut; First Congregational Church in New Milford, Connecticut; and Silver Lake Conference Center in Connecticut. We are grateful for the help, inspiration and support of the people in the United Church of Gainesville, who have planned and shared retreats with us for the past twelve years.

We offer a special thanks to Steve Wilburn of Morehouse-Barlow for his understanding of retreats, for his belief in us, and for his good humor.

Introduction

Like most people who grew up participating in church life, we both had significant adolescent faith experiences on youth group retreats. Those times of being away from home in a group setting included experiences of individual prayer at morning watch, lighting candles of commitment at lakeside communion, and sharing important issues in discussion groups. Our retreats also included plenty of recreation, talent shows, and mealtimes which probably filled us with more fun than food. The mingling of friendship and faith, of laughter and contemplation, was a mixture in which we discovered who we were and what we believed. Each of us experienced those times separately, in different places. But we remember those retreats as important, exciting events in our lives and in our religious foundations.

It was quite natural that, when we began working in churches ourselves, we offered retreat experiences for the young people. We believed that retreats offered them some of the best opportunities for the development of an individual's faith. We then realized that we were holding these retreats not just for the young people but for ourselves. Our faith was nurtured again in these same kinds of experiences. The other adults who helped with these youth group overnights said the same thing. So why didn't we do retreats for the adults in the church?

That question got us started. The retreat experience seemed to be an important waystation on the lifelong journey of faith. We decided to try an adult retreat, knowing that we were going to learn as we did it. At this time we were Associate Pastor and Youth Director of a large New England church that had not tried an adult retreat before.

We found a site, got commitments from some interested people, put the sign-up sheet on the bulletin board and started planning. Some people signed up, but the list stayed very empty. As the date approached, a few more names appeared on the list with much encouragement from us. Then one week before the retreat, we felt like the host in Jesus' parable of the great feast in Luke 14. Excuses poured in. No one could come. Unlike the host in Jesus' parable, we cancelled.

We regrouped again the next year. This time we decided to include children, since child care difficulties were a primary reason people gave for not coming the year before. We recruited ten families of different varieties to make a firm commitment before we posted the sign-up sheet. All the church staff, including the senior pastor, were scheduled to participate, and all helped recruit church members.

About fifty adults and children went on the first retreat at a place called Bish Bash Falls in upstate New York. Our planning was rather primitive, as were the surroundings. We began like honeymooners who weren't quite sure how to act with each other on this first big trip. But all of a sudden, there we were, singing in front of the fireplace in the evening, and we began bonding as a group. There was lots of free time that weekend, as well as lots of time spent preparing and cleaning up from meals. The children had fun together. And, the morning before we went home, we met outside by the lake, sharing a prayer in a circle. Barriers between people had fallen, and there was a new trust and joy within the group.

That church still holds a spring family retreat, fifteen years later. The format changes. Different people come and go, but the retreat continues as a part of adult faith development.

We moved from that church after the second year of family retreats. When we arrived in Florida, we discovered the all-church retreat. Our new church closed its doors one weekend every spring, and the entire membership was invited to go away for Saturday and Sunday. The retreat was scheduled a month after our arrival, so we attended as participants, not leaders. About sixty people, including children, came to the retreat.

The site was a cross between real north Florida beauty and a primitive mining camp. There were live oak trees covered with Spanish moss, a lodge with a big stone fireplace and a swimming pool. There were also concrete block cabins laid out in rows, with hard cement floors, surrounded by more dirt than grass. Our own experience reflected the same highs and lows of the surroundings. Instead of breaking into small discussion groups, the forty adults tried to discuss everything together. Little was planned for younger children other than for them to spend the day in a giant sandpile. It looked like it might be a bad situation. But then that spirit started flowing which enlivens and enables retreats. Small groups did finally break off for sharing. Living in a cabin with another family who also had small children and babies produced a bond which we still share as two families that now have teenage children.

Each retreat has special turning points. On this one, some of us gathered under a tree at night after all the organized activities were over. We talked and shared, joking, challenging, and caring, for several hours. We formed a circle with our arms around each other, looking up at the stars and felt a presence, the holy among us, a bond of fellowship. We stayed out under those stars, afraid to break the beauty of that moment until it started raining on us hard enough to chase us into our cabins.

That was twelve years ago. This church has held an all-church retreat every year since then. The turning point moments have been different in each of them. This last year one of the men who stood in that circle we described in our first Florida retreat returned to our church retreat after four years' absence. He had been divorced and had moved out of town. He wrote that coming back for such an event filled him with all kinds of anxiety and apprehension, but there it was again, the warmth, fellowship, and most of all, the grace of acceptance that he had found on the first retreat.

We work together in this church: Sandy as the program director and Larry as the pastor. We often run youth group and small group adult overnights together. When it is time for our all-church retreat, Sandy is the retreat coordinator, organizing and supervising the entire event. Larry participates as the clergy resource person, coordinating the worship components of the retreat. We have grown professionally through fifteen years of retreat experience; we have also grown personally as adults in these experiences. Each year we have discovered something new for ourselves, our church, our faith on these retreats. Communion late at night in a room lit just with candles has opened us to the power of sharing the joys and struggles of our lives. Talent shows have given us the grace of laughter. Each year we have learned something new in a challenging discussion group. And every year there has been a time when we found ourselves talking quietly with just one other person in a conversation which has opened up a new dimension in both our lives. We have understood each other more fully in the marriage groups. We have watched our children grow from infants being held by supportive friends to teenagers who are still guided by our supportive friends who now supervise the youth activities rather than feed them cereal.

Why is a retreat so special? Two notions come to mind. The first is suggested by Tilden Edwards of the Shalem Institute in Washington, D.C. He describes his own pilgrimage as a religious activist committed to living his faith through social change. At one point he noticed the symptoms of burnout in his life and the way his family life was becoming rather raw. He sensed a need for a different rhythm in life and found it in the recovery of sabbath. He initiated a regular time for his family to have sabbath moments: a special meal, time to share stories, time unbothered by outside influences. From there he suggested that the primary task for the church in the next decade would be to recover a rhythm of sabbath: a time for reflection, celebration, withdrawal, and renewal for ministry to the world. (*All God's Children,* Abingdon, 1983.)

The retreat is one way for the church family to have a time of sabbath, an opportunity to experience God's grace as acceptance. Sabbath time must be set aside from the routine of life. It must be time when you can wait and be open to receive God's spirit. Good sabbath and good retreats then send you back into the world renewed to your commitments, values, and ministries. The retreat experience cannot be duplicated in regular morning worship anymore than sabbath can be replicated at work. The retreat is a unique gift of the spirit, part of the necessary rhythm and balance of faith.

A second reason the retreat seems so important is suggested by *Habits of the Heart,* a study of individuals and commitment in American life edited by Robert Bellah (University of California Press, 1985). The authors of this book see Americans experiencing a split between their public and private lives which is difficult to bridge. Both arenas are good and important, but there are few places where public and private values are bridged. As a result people find themselves isolated and alone. There are public values at work and private values at home. One of the only institutions able to help an individual express private values in a public setting is the church.

The retreat is a place where an individual can explore and share the significant and most private "habits of the heart" in a context of community support. Each of us has deep questions, fears of being lost, wonderings about what we are doing here in this place at this time. We think about the mysteries of our lives, but the people we work with are not necessarily the ones to share those questions. And even the normal routines of church do not often lend themselves to opening the questions of the soul.

The retreat lets everyone raise those questions, "Who am I?" "What does God ask of me?" "How can I respond and find a life of meaning?" Then the retreat offers the opportunity, away from normal tasks, for the care, the time, the support, and the silence to consider these questions. The private realm of the soul and the public sphere of the community are bridged. Retreats become indelible memories in the soul. We can easily identify those memories in individual retreats we have experienced. But when the whole church shares these retreats, they become part of the communal memory of the soul of the church itself.

We share these retreat experiences because we believe they are essential to the soul of the church and to our personal souls as well. They are also times of ministry which we both enjoy and treasure. While retreats take time and effort to plan, they are a source of incredible energy and reward. We love to plan them; we love to participate in them; we love to share them. We have grown together with the church communities and the individual people who have shared their retreats with us over the years. We in turn offer them to you as an opportunity for personal growth and enjoyment, as a way to balance ministry with sabbath, and as a bridge to the personal habits of the heart.

The Retreat Handbook

Section I
The All-Church Retreat

Introduction

A retreat made available to everyone in the church is unique among church experiences. From the youngest babies, to the oldest members, the whole church is invited to an experience of community and renewal in a time away. The key to the all-church retreat is that facilities, program, and theme apply to everyone in the church. Every church member does not have to attend to make it an all-church retreat; it simply needs to be open to everyone. This distinguishes it from other retreats which focus on specific groups within the church.

This openness to and involvement of everyone is important. Often a retreat advertised for the whole church is directed at adults with young children and the rest of the community is asked to tag along. If, however, the program embraces the physical as well as the spiritual and emotional needs of all ages, then it can be called an all-church retreat.

The benefits of such a retreat resonate throughout the church the whole year long. No matter how many small group retreats a church may run during the year, such experiences inevitably divide up families and friends. People are always excluded. Benefit number one is that when the whole church is invited, the message is communicated from the start that this is a time for the whole community to be gathered.

It is still inevitable that some church members will not be able to attend. No matter how inclusive the organizational design, there will be some people who cannot participate because of business conflicts, health reasons, or other obligations. Their issues need to be remembered. For example, Sunday morning worship should be held at the retreat. This makes it clear that church is a movable feast not a stationary building. Buses or car pools can be set up to bring people to the retreat site. People who cannot take advantage of this opportunity can be encouraged to visit another church of their choice, a good experience in and of itself. But the symbol of the all-church retreat still remains intact.

Benefit number two is that an all-church retreat gets people away from their normal routines. We often get just as tied to our weekend routines as to our weekday routines. To be able to leave lawn care, soccer games, gymnastics classes, and other social and recreational responsibilities is a great leap of freedom. Sometimes the most significant event at a church retreat is the moment everyone has finally arrived, unpacked, gathered, and exhaled; they see that they have in fact let goods, if not kindred, go and are all there together.

Benefit number three is that community then develops on a level impossible in normal church routines. Sleeping together is quite a bond. Eating together can be almost sacramental. Taking the time for discussion offers learning opportunities impossible in Sunday School or class times. I am always amazed at the sense of freedom in staying up far past my normal bed time to share communion at midnight, walk by the lake, or sing into the morning. These are the indelible elements of community that rise naturally at a retreat.

There are also the more difficult but equally important aspects of community. Working together to plan the event, bringing in the supplies, keeping the machinery running, and cleaning up after the event all develop community. But perhaps most difficult and most important is benefit number four—the experience of sticking with people you didn't absolutely choose to be with. The church, especially on a retreat, is like an extended family. There are always people in the church, just as there are in our families, whom we would not choose to live with.

The nature of the spiritual experience of an all-church retreat is an interesting fifth benefit. The spiritual intensity of an all-church retreat may not always be the same as a small group experience. Distractions are present, so the spiritual experiences, while heightened, still include reminders of outside world. In ways this is healthier than the mountaintop experiences of the intensive small group retreat.

Benefit number six is the celebration of play and fun as part of the church experience. When we were traveling a few summers ago, we stayed at a motel outside Yosemite National Park. This motel was built next to an old logging railroad, and part of the Saturday night experience was a cookout and ride on an old train to a campfire in the woods where a guitarist led the group in singing. Families paid as much for that two-hour experience as they pay for a typical weekend church retreat. The food, train ride and singing were good, but not great, because there was no real opportunity to build that group into a community.

I was struck by the hunger these people had for the kind of experience the church can readily offer on a retreat, the chance to just enjoy themselves in a community at a meal around a fire in the evening. We should never underestimate the simple gifts of fun that a retreat offers.

Finally, the church itself gains strength from this kind of retreat. Beyond the benefits to individuals who attend, the body of the church is renewed and refreshed. The church is experienced in a different setting, away from its usual identification with building and ritual. For the rest of the year, members refer to retreat experiences in living out the mission of church.

Chapter 1

How to Get Started

This is the hardest part of the all-church retreat. While people talk constantly about wanting to go away on a retreat, when it comes to actually doing it, the excuses of the invited guests at Jesus' parable of the great wedding feast pale compared to the reasons church folk give as to why they can't attend. It is good to recognize that resistance always precedes growth. The growth offered in a retreat naturally triggers resistance. There are a number of different ways of working through resistance to get a retreat started.

First, identify a core group that will commit themselves to the retreat. As we will see, this is a rule for every type of retreat. But in an all-church retreat where it may seem like there is no single group responsible, it is crucial to begin this way. These should be people who enjoy each other and who will have a good experience even if few others attend the first retreat. It would be best if this group represented a good cross section of the church, but if there is no such group willing to make this commitment, then two or three groups may have to be gathered to get it started. You are already bridging the resistance by offering mutual support.

The danger here, of course, is that the rest of the church may assume that the retreat is really for this group only. Therefore it is necessary to move out of that core group in assembling a planning committee. It is best if an all-church retreat is not planned by an existing church board. First, they have their own work to do, and second they do represent a specific segment of church work.

Gather an ad hoc task force to plan the retreat, one made of people who represent singles, couples, longtime members, new members, young members, people with small children, teenagers, and older people. If possible, there should be people on this task force who have had good retreat experiences themselves.

It may seem strange, but for the first retreat this group should be gathered for an initial meeting about 13 months prior to a targeted retreat date. It may not be necessary to have the whole retreat committee in place this soon, but at least three or four key people need to gather to set a date and find a site.

Chapter 2
Selecting the Site

I t is important to recognize that most conference centers do schedule a year in advance. Many groups get excited about a retreat, gather a committee, and then discover that no quality retreat facility is available to them. By giving yourself just over a year to plan your first retreat, you can take a month to gather possibilities, visit sites, and make your reservation early enough to find an excellent place.

Before looking for a site, outline what you want in a retreat center. It is important to involve your cross-section of membership in this first brainstorming session for a retreat site. The first retreat enthusiasts to come forward usually look for a rustic, camplike setting. These are folks comfortable with camping and often have been involved with scouting. Our experience, however, is that the very rustic setting is also what makes it difficult for a retreat to be truly inclusive. The second and third level of people interested in retreats may be hesitant to speak up at first, but they are often the ones who would prefer a conference-style facility.

Look for both kinds of sites, rustic and comfortable (we may betray a small bias here), and look at the pros and cons of each. It may be that your group freely and by consensus chooses a rustic setting for the first retreat. We have been involved in such retreats, and they were very good. But make sure you have looked at other options as well.

Do you want to have food prepared for you? Cooking together can be a great source of fellowship, but it also adds tremendously to the work both for the committee and the participants. On the retreat, the people preparing and cleaning up after meals will not be able to participate in retreat programs for at least an hour before and after each meal. Our recommendation is to go where food is prepared or arrange for a cook and crew to come along. For the first all-church retreat, put as few obstacles as possible in the way of people coming and fully participating.

Secondly, look at the sleeping facilities. The best sites have variety. In our church, we look for cabins of 12-15 bunks to sleep families with children of similar ages. We then like two cabins for high school boys and girls. We need cabins for single adults, and then we want individual rooms for people with small babies and for older people or anyone with special health needs who would find it difficult to sleep bunk style.

Consider how your church would best arrange itself. You may put two or three families together in cabins, and let them work out ways to dress and divide up restrooms. Or you may want to divide up men and women dorm style. Just don't assume that all small children will stay with the women, or you will begin your retreat with a guaranteed conflict.

Next look at what kind of meeting and recreational space you want. What will you do in case of rain? Where can the whole community gather? Is there a bonfire site for vespers or singing? Is there a lake? It may not be swimming season, but a lake, like a bonfire, always has gathering power.

How far do you want to travel? Ideally, you want to be far enough away so that people do not run back and forth for meetings, children's sports activities, or to catch up on some work. But you don't want to go so far that the distance works against you. If you can find a site within an hour to an hour and a half drive, this would be perfect. Unless there is just no other way to do it, a drive of over two hours can work against your goals.

Estimate the minimum and maximum numbers you would expect, and then begin contacting retreat and conference centers.

Your first resource is your own denominational office. But don't use their camp or conference center out of denominational loyalty. It may be in the wrong place and not set up in a way that meets your needs at all. If that is true, ask your denominational staff person in charge of camps and conferences for names of other sites.

Utilize the references of friends in other churches. Ask them where they go, and then check out their sites with other churches and denominational centers. Also contact the YMCA and your state council of churches. Usually one of these organizations publishes a guide of facilities.

Call with specific questions about facilities, and then have a delegation visit the site. Get prices and find out availability of dates.

Discuss your options. Imagine what it would be like to be at these places for your retreat. Make your choice, set your date, check out all the details of the contract. Then take some good pictures and do your first publicizing.

Chapter 3
Publicity

P ublicity occurs in two phases. While most of it will occur near the retreat, the first publicity should start almost a year in advance. If you want your whole church to participate in this event, you will need time to make this idea part of the thinking of the whole church. People need to think "retreat" like they think Christmas and Easter.

This is truly sabbath time, and other church events should not conflict with it. No choir concerts, youth group parties, or Sunday school outings should be held on or near the retreat date. Part of publicity is church scheduling, keeping everything clear.

One good poster should be placed on a visible bulletin board as soon as possible, even if this is a year in advance. The pictures you took of the retreat site should be there. The dates should be large, and an encouraging word should be included.

The planning committee for the retreat should start meeting in earnest four months prior to the retreat to set a theme. Develop a good logo to go along with the theme and start adding new posters with the logo all around the church. Use the logo with all printed material relating to the retreat.

Two months prior to the retreat, start distributing specific information about cost, place, date, and theme. Use whatever meetings are convenient to share plans for the retreat. Adult Sunday school classes, children's Sunday school, youth group meetings, and weekday study groups are all places where retreat committee members should speak, conveying information about the retreat as well as their own enthusiasm. Make these announcements creative and fun. Show slides, share stories of special retreat experiences from the past and help people visualize what this experience will mean for themselves and for the church. Feature the retreat as a lead article in the newsletter for several months. It is worthwhile to take two to three minutes in the time for sharing announcements and concerns of the church during morning worship to have committee members communicate their excitement about the coming retreat.

This is also a time for the original committed core to begin making personal invitations to others. For a first retreat, this may be the most crucial part of publicity. There is a good deal of anxiety about going off to an unknown event for the first time, and the best antidote for that anxiety is a personal invitation with a promise of support on the retreat itself.

Chapter 4
Organization and Planning

We have covered the need for advance planning above. When you are not dealing with the first all-church retreat, the outgoing retreat committee can often make the long-term arrangements for next year's retreat. We will conclude this section with arrangements for next year. At this point we can assume that the date has been set and the site selected.

An all-church retreat committee represents all the church. Thus, our vision of this kind of retreat includes all ages and a variety of family types. The retreat committee membership must reflect the various age groups, interests, and lifestyles of the congregation as a whole. Weaknesses and omissions in the program will directly parallel weaknesses and omissions in the retreat committee. As the all-church retreat grows, it will become clear that you are running three to four retreats in one. You will have programs and activities for children, youth, and adults, plus differentiated programs for singles, couples, younger and older adults. Always, however, the community will regather as one.

The first step is for key staff and lay leaders to consider an organizational design for the committee. Obviously, the smaller the church, the more activities which the whole group can plan together. The larger the church, the more subgroups which will need organization. The committee should reflect the size and design of the retreat.

Within this design process is the consideration of who will be the facilitator for the whole retreat. Leadership of a retreat of up to 125 participants can be handled by a church lay leader with active support of professional staff. When the retreat becomes larger than that, the job of leading becomes too big for most volunteers.

Whether volunteer or paid staff member, the leader has to be relieved of other church responsibilities during this time and given as much backup support as the church can provide. Then the committee can be selected.

This is a time to discern the gifts of the congregation. Skills for retreat leadership are different from traditional church boards. Celebrate new opportunities for involvement in retreats.

The retreat committee for a small retreat can be a group of people who meet together and plan all of the components. For a larger retreat each committee member should have a specific area of responsibility. The committee as a whole does overall planning and coordinating, but the details are left to each person's individual area. We suggest the following divisions of responsibility: a recreation person to organize games for a variety of interests and ages; two to four people for adult programming; a high-school leader; a middle or junior high leader; a leader for elementary school children (or two if you need to break this group down); a leader for preschool children; a coordinator for small child care, and a registrar. Clergy should meet with the committee as a resource person, taking leadership of worship experiences.

These committee members are not necessarily the people who will run programs for each of these areas. They are coordinators who will recruit and schedule others to do the games, discussion groups, and children's activities. Other special events that become part of the retreat tradition might also have a representative on the committee. For example, a retreat is a great place for a variety show, and the convener of that program should also sit on the committee. A person in charge of evaluation is another resource for the retreat committee, as would be a songleader.

The retreat committee may meet as a whole only three or four times. In between full committee meetings, individual members will be gathering their own teams to take care of their special tasks. The purpose of the full committee meetings is to set the theme, make sure all activities are coordinated, and help each other fill in gaps.

At the first meeting the leader gives an overview of what happens on an all-church retreat. Either an organizational structure of a previous retreat or a suggested design can be distributed so that committee members have an idea of where they fit in. Models of sample retreats at the end of this section could be used here. The key is to find that balance between providing enough of a framework so that the committee does not feel lost and not so much structure so that they feel overwhelmed or trapped.

Let there be some sharing to build the trust level and consolidate the group. Food, by the way, is a wonderful bonding experience. Beginning the first meeting with a simple meal in a comfortable setting gives the group a great start.

Then move to picking a theme for the retreat. Sometimes the key leadership may have something very specific in mind, and the group might pick this right up. Other times the theme will flow from the group itself. Start by letting people brainstorm the kind of experiences they are looking forward to on the retreat. Remember the rules of brainstorming are that every idea is accepted, nothing is criticized, and every suggestion is written down. Encourage everyone to offer some input, and welcome any kind of suggestion from something as specific as the need for a softball game to as general as a desire for time to share.

After a while, common themes will emerge. You should see a general sense of the mood of the church in that year. Sometimes people will feel the need for challenge and stimulation; other times you will see a specific need for rest and nurture.

Look for a general theme that would unite the concerns before you. Be aware of contemporary themes of the era or the larger church. "Leaps" once emerged as a leap year theme suggesting everything from discussion groups on "Leaps of Faith" to an all-age field day called "O'leapics." The beginning of a decade lends itself to futuristic visions as every popular periodical seems to engage in every ten years.

It is amazing to watch a theme come from a group. Both of us worry that no one will have any ideas, so we typically come with ready-made themes. Committee members, however, always develop their own themes, which fit the needs of the church quite well.

The role of the leader is to keep the theme broad enough so that it can enable all kinds of experiences and learning. For example, a very responsible retreat committee might decide that this is the year to do a retreat on world hunger. That is an admirable goal, as would be a retreat on the ten commandments, or the theology of Paul Tillich. This is a place for the leader to place any of these concerns that seem to be on minds of the whole group under a larger umbrella. World hunger could be part of a theme of "Spaceship Earth" or "To Care for One Another." Concern for the ten commandments could be dealt with under a theme of "Roles and Rules." What would you do with Tillich—perhaps "Grounds and Beings"?

Part of the theme should be to make sure that the weekend is fun. Church people get serious enough. Fun is a gift to give and an integral part of a successful retreat. Don't let the retreat committee get too heavy.

We often feel that the test of a good theme is how much energy it generates. If a theme is suggested, and no ideas about activities follow quickly, then it is probably not a good theme. However, if someone suggests a theme, and two or three others begin talking about a discussion group and a children's activity that can focus on that theme, then the idea is giving energy to the group.

Once a theme has been chosen, the retreat coordinator should hand out a previously prepared time schedule for the retreat with some suggestions of obvious events already listed. A sample follows.

PRELIMINARY TIME SCHEDULE

FRIDAY NIGHT
5:30–7:30	Registration
8:00	Bonfire and singing
9:30	Adult Activity
10:30	Communion

SATURDAY
8:00	Breakfast
9:00–10:30	Adult Workshops
12:00	Lunch
1:15–2:45	Adult Workshops
6:00	Dinner
8:15	Talent Show

SUNDAY
8:00	Breakfast
9:00–10:30	Adult Workshops
11:00	Worship Service
12:00	Lunch
2:30	Campground closes

This preliminary schedule should include: starting time, registration, meals, and check-out time. The retreat committee can then begin to fill in events and activities which they want to add. This preliminary schedule should be a broad general framework which can be changed or rearranged during the next committee meeting if necessary. It is an important step because it allows committee members to begin to visualize what the time at the retreat will be like. It also avoids putting the whole committee through a tedious discussion of when to schedule meals.

The committee can then focus briefly on each area of responsibility and brainstorm suggestions and concerns for each leader. For instance, everyone would give ideas to the adult program subcommittee about what discussion topics they would like, resource people, and whether they would want a keynote speaker. The pros and cons of a keynote speaker are important to consider. Some committees get excited about the possibility of outside input. Other committees prefer to use small discussion groups to handle a theme. Preferences change from year to year. Take the time to gather data from the committee on this issue. In the same way, everyone on the committee will then take the time to give suggestions for the other areas of responsibility, such as children's activities, recreation, and worship.

Give each person on the committee a written list of their responsibilities including a timetable of when to get them done. This list should be informational and helpful in tone, dealing with broad categories of responsibility.

The retreat chairperson, in conjunction with the church staff, can compile a list of resource people for each committee person to call upon to staff his or her activities. These should be people who do not have current intense responsibilities in the regular organizational structure of the church. By dividing and designating volunteers in this way, you avoid committee members calling the same people or people already overloaded with church jobs. If someone wants a choice from another committee member's list, they then trade names, like the National Football League draft! Nothing wears out recruiters or burns out volunteers like calling people who are already committed or being called over and over again. This step is essential to save wear and tear on your volunteers. An alternative option to staffing activities is to develop your schedule in detail first and then make a sign-up list showing clearly where you need volunteers. As people register for the retreat, they are asked to volunteer for one of the jobs on the sign up list. This avoids a lot of phone calling, but it probably works best once the congregation has had several retreat experiences so that people are familiar with a retreat schedule and have some sense of the jobs to be done.

Before concluding this meeting, emphasize the importance of activities for children and young people. It's easy to give primary importance to adult programs and treat young people's activities as time fillers. However, activities for children and young people serve purposes beyond baby sitting. First, they give the young people a powerful and positive retreat experience themselves. Attendance at the kind of summer church conferences many of today's adults experienced as young people is declining. This all-church retreat may be the primary retreat experience for today's young people. Secondly, if the young people are having a good experience, their parents' experience will be enhanced. Whether a child is four or fourteen, if that child is excited, stimulated, and looking forward to his or her activities, the retreat will be a better experience for the parents.

Have the committee consider the entry to the retreat as well. This is a very important time, and it is good to get input from the whole committee about how the retreat begins. If you are starting on a Friday evening, it will take a while for people to arrive and check in. Establish a time when everyone is expected to be there. Begin with some icebreaker activities, things which help people relax and learn something about each other. Being involved in something active can help ease any initial discomfort or anxiety. Samples of entry icebreakers are listed in the Appendix.

With these understandings made clear, set the date for the next committee meeting. When each person has the theme, a preliminary time frame, suggestions for activities in their area, and people they can call to help them with their area, the meeting can be adjourned. Committee members disperse for several weeks to develop their own programs and gather key people to lead them. At this stage, the emphasis is on developing the program, not on fully staffing activities.

The importance of this design is that it covers the whole experience of the retreat. In our experience with our first retreat, we spent most of the time planning adult discussion topics and worship. This takes up a relatively small portion of the time on the retreat. It was the retreat as a whole that impacted on people's lives. They talked about running together, singing late at night, playing with the children, meditating in the morning, just walking with a friend and talking. How a volleyball game is organized and how time is facilitated for people to find each other for quiet sharing are just as important as topics for Bible study or theological discussion. This has to be emphasized regularly to all retreat members. A retreat is not just a time for a keynote speaker or group discussion with recreational and social activities thrown in. Every element is a gift of the spirit with equal importance.

By now individual committee members are developing ways to weave their activities into the theme of the retreat. For example, a retreat that will be described more fully later is "A Rainbow of Diversity: Family Lifestyles." An opening activity for adults and children in that retreat involved drawing a symbolic family tree. At another time small children did a nature walk exploring animal and plant families. Middle schoolers played their own version of "Family Feud." High schoolers were each given an egg to care for as if it were their child, for the whole weekend. The adult committee invited a keynote speaker from the family life priority of the denomination and followed her address with topics such as "Breaking Away," "Who Cleans the Toilet? Finding a New Balance in Household Roles," and "Waiting for the Messiah: Exploring Spirituality in the Family."

With some ideas in mind, committee members begin recruiting activity leaders. Most leadership can come from within the congregation. And recruited leaders can tailor programs to their talents.

Here is an opportunity to look at the debate of inside and outside leadership. Most churches look first for an outside resource person to keynote a retreat. They also tend to look for outside leaders for discussion groups. However, churches generally find that when they trust the gifts within the congregation, church members often do as well if not better in facilitating good experiences. Church members know the congregation. They know the concerns and history of the group. They may be shy, even hesitant about leadership, but with some basic training they can generally lead a group out of their own experience.

Outside leadership is a calculated risk. We have seen both the best and the worst leadership come from outsiders. The best outside leaders were people whom we had seen and heard in similar group situations. The worst were those we had simply heard about. Be careful of blind invitations to people who are supposed to be good.

About a week before the next committee meeting, send reminders to the members with a sense of what will be on the agenda. At this meeting you will focus on developing a semifinal schedule of events, and to do this each program leader will need to know what activities they want to schedule. At the meeting you will adjust times and activities so that there is a good progression of events. Walk the committee through the schedule mentally. Consider how one event flows into another and if there is enough time to get from one place to another. A good rule of thumb is to always add ten more minutes for transition than you think you need.

Close this meeting by asking if anything has been overlooked. Is any group overloaded or underscheduled? This is where the individual committee members give each other a sense of perspective. Establish a deadline for all information that is to be included on the retreat schedule.

If plans are flowing smoothly, the next step is to be sure that all the helpers are recruited and in place to staff activities. You should only need one more brief meeting to make sure that everything is set, just prior to the retreat itself.

Chapter 5

Suggestions for Committee Members

A *dult programming.* Once a theme is established, the adult program committee has the important task of designing discussions and experiences for adult growth and learning. Begin with establishing a balance of biblical/religious, personal growth, and social issues.

To get a sense of what is on people's minds at the moment, scan the bestseller list of fiction and nonfiction books. Note the themes present there. Consider the current spiritual issues of people in the congregation. If you are not sure of the burning questions for your church, survey key people. As planners for the adult program, trust your own instincts. Ask yourselves what kind of groups you would like to attend.

When you set up groups, every leader should know that the purpose of the groups is discussion, not lecturing. Distribute basic guidelines for group leadership. Find out what kind of space and supplies each group needs. Most of all, communicate to the group leaders that the retreat is to be a safe place for people to be both challenged and nurtured.

Balance the groups between heavy and lightweight material. While one group might study the theme of a current book, another might gather to sing or do needlework. Allow right-brain, intuitive, experiential groups as well as left-brain, intellectual, verbal activities. Whenever you schedule a program segment, go over an imaginary list of those who will be present and see if any group of people is left out at that time.

A retreat can offer an opportunity for couples to meet together to look at a marriage issue. This should be done carefully, but it can be very simple. Couples can be gathered by a person with some training in counselling (here it may be good to invite a resource person), and given some very basic and nurturing topics to discuss. For example, married partners may each make a collage out of magazine photos which represents their marriage. They then go aside as couples and discuss them with each other, returning to share feelings and discoveries with the group. Activities need be no more intense or elaborate than this. In a casual setting in the midst of a retreat, keep the marriage emphasis positive.

At the same time there have to be activities for singles. Scheduling this so that the retreat is not suddenly split totally between married and single people is tricky. One way to do this is to offer the marriage group more than one time with other groups always available.

In all groups offered for adult programs, the key test is whether you find them enjoyable. If so, you can trust that others will as well.

High School leader. What your high school group does will depend largely on the size of your group. Even if only a few high school students attend, specific activities have to be offered for them. This may be a time to have people work with high school young people who do not meet with them regularly during the rest of the year. You will need a good balance between fun and seriousness. Many of the activities need to be physical. Often the high schoolers will enjoy challenging another group to something like a volleyball or softball game.

An ongoing theme or connection with the retreat theme can work very well. High school students will work better if they feel separated from the rest of the group and have some privacy during part of the time and yet have activities which connect them back with the larger community at various points in the weekend. Participating in the talent show or having a part in one of the worship services are two ways to make this connection. It is also important to keep their tremendous appetites in mind and have regular snacks.

They love late-night activities, either listening to records or making a huge snack. And it is often possible to affirm their growing maturity by offering late-night communion by the fireside or lake with opportunities for important sharing.

Middle Schoolers. While this group may sometimes seem a bit overwhelming to consider working with, they can also be the most rewarding. Keep in mind their tremendous energy and their desire to perform. Middle schoolers spend their lives imagining an invisible audience for their every move. Thus role plays, acts they can perform for the larger group, and simulations work well. They are a natural group to participate in a talent show.

This group never sits still long, so mix up every sitting activity with a physical activity. Remember how important it is for them to have fun together in a church setting. Keep in mind that they are just this side of adolescence and just that side of childhood. Sometimes they will enjoy playing younger games. Sometimes they will enjoy copying older activities. Let them do both.

Elementary school children. These children love being on retreats. They are just free enough of their parents to think this is wonderful, but their parents are accessible enough to keep them from feeling the confusion and homesickness of being away at camp. They enjoy activities such as crafts, scavenger hunts, nature walks, kickball, collages, and soccer. Older elementary children can work on a retreat newspaper. Give them story assignments and interviews with teenagers and adults. Polaroid pictures, sports specials, spiritual questionnaires can all be part of a newspaper posted at every meal.

Remember that the children are away and need to have fun. Biblical explorations can be simulations of Bible journeys. Sharing and personal growth can be very tender at this age. Again, keep them physically active.

Preschool children. Find someone with nursery school skills to coordinate these activities. Keep the children safe and comfortable. Vary the leadership and activities to prevent burnout in the adults. Remember to have rest time for these small children. This is a wonderful opportunity for telling Bible stories. The primary task will be to make these children feel secure enough so that parents can be comfortable in leaving them.

Babysitter coordinator. If you want families with young children (under three) to participate in the retreat, bring along paid babysitters. If your nursery uses hired sitters, bring them if possible. The children, parents, and sitters then already know and trust each other. Parents of this age group need a break and will be better able to participate in the adult activities.

You will have to sketch out carefully just how much child care you can provide and stick with it. Hire enough sitters so that there is a good ratio of sitters to children for the babies and toddlers. Sitters can also be used to check in on children at night, freeing the parents to be a part of evening activities.

Good child care is probably the best investment of the whole retreat budget.

Recreation coordinator. The recreation coordinator's role is to help people have fun. It is important to clarify from the beginning whether this person will be in charge of sports alone or will also oversee the welcoming and group building activities which start the retreat. Whether the recreation person or someone connected with adult programming will handle entry activities will depend upon the skills of the people involved and the wishes of the retreat committee. Determine early whose job this will be.

For the rest of the weekend, get a sense of how your group likes to play. If you've got a lot of joggers, set up a time for a fun run when all can run together. If you do competitive games like softball or soccer, keep mixing up the teams, even change the rules if necessary, to avoid slaughters! Field day events, relays, etc. are good ways to involve different ages.

During times for recreation, make sure there are activities appropriate for all ages, from kickball for the little ones to board games for folks who want to sit. Encourage individuals to gather groups for volleyball or other sports. Utilize the waterfront if available, and don't overorganize. Give people a chance to relax and enjoy themselves as well.

Ham it up. Get a whistle. Rent an electric bullhorn. Put on a pith helmet. Let people know you are making things happen. Then help them organize themselves.

If your group is small, you can change the rules to play many games that usually involve large teams. One bounce volleyball can be played with three people on a side. Softball with one base and any ball fair works too. Just let your imagination roll.

Registrar. Keeping the accounts of the number of people registered and the money collected is a big job. The registrar begins by working with the camp or conference center in determining what fees the camp will charge. They may break down charges by ages, and this should be reflected in the cost to the congregation. There are always other expenses to consider as well. The camp may have a flat rate for waterfront usage, lifeguard, snacks, etc. which you must prorate per member. Then the committee itself will generate certain costs such as supplies, outside speakers, babysitters, or even extra food.

The registrar must prepare a fee schedule for the retreat which has ample room for cancellations and unexpected expenses. Then you need to determine a reasonable deposit and method of payment with a clear stipulation of what is refundable in the event of cancellation. Design a method for registration with specific times for reservations to begin and end. Gather the volunteers you will need to help with the registration process.

Arrange with the church treasurer for the handling of income and payments, and develop an in-and-out retreat account in the church budget. Explore the possibility of scholarship funds for those who need them. It is often possible to do some fundraising for scholarships in the off season through activities like suppers or garage sales. There may be individuals the pastor knows who would contribute toward this fund to help those who cannot afford the full retreat cost. Some families may need to spread their payments out over several months. A scholarship fund can provide loan money for these individuals who will then repay it to the scholarship account.

Once this scholarship money is in place, you can make it clear that no one needs to stay home because of financial concerns. Obviously, tact and discretion should be used. The people who need scholarship or loan money must be assured of the confidentiality of such arrangements.

Develop a clear registration form. This form should include:
- the dates, place, and theme of the retreat, including beginning and ending times.
- a statement which welcomes everyone, regardless of age or marital status.
- information about fees and about the scholarship and loan money.
- any policy about children or young people attending without their parents. (Our policy is that any person under 18 years of age must have an adult sponsor at the retreat.)
- deadlines and refund policy.
- a place to sign up all family members. It is helpful to have the children and young people identified here both by age and grade.
- a place to indicate a preference for someone you want to be in a cabin with.

There should also be an information sheet available at the time of registration that gives people as much information about the

event as possible so that their questions are answered and their anxiety is reduced. The information sheet should answer in detail:
- Where is the retreat held?
- What are the directions for getting there?
- What are the facilities like? Be sure to have data here about sleeping arrangements, bathrooms, showers, and recreational facilities.
- What is the theme of the retreat?
- What is the schedule like? It is good to include some suggestions in this part, such as: "You will receive a complete schedule when you arrive on Friday evening. Please take some time to read through the schedule and make plans about what you want to do. If you want to have some special time with a child, a spouse, or a friend, you may need to make specific arrangements for that, as the weekend goes by very quickly. Try to think about what you need personally from the retreat, and choose activities which focus on those needs. It is your weekend and we want you to enjoy it."
- What happens to the children during the weekend?
- What clothes should I bring?
- What else should I know? This is a good place to include information about any camp rules, such as "smoking is not permitted inside any building. Food is not allowed in the cabins. The camp does not allow alcoholic beverages. Please lock valuables in the trunk of your car."

We recommend that you begin registration three or four weeks prior to the retreat. Set up a table in a visible, accessible place in your church on Sunday mornings. Provide an alternative means of registering for people who cannot be there on Sundays.

Most retreat centers require a final count of people five to seven days prior to the event. Have those numbers prepared in time, and give a master list to the retreat coordinator. Information on the number of children and adults who are attending is very helpful to the various leaders in each area as they make their final plans. Determine cabin assignments with the retreat coordinator.

Plan to arrive at least an hour before check-in on the day of the retreat. Have some volunteers who will greet people on their arrival and show them to their cabins. Middle and high school young people can often be very good in these roles. As people arrive, have a clearly marked place for them to sign in. A map of the retreat center should be included in the program booklet. Post the list of cabin assignments so that people can find each other. Have a provision for latecomers to sign in, and keep an accurate count of attendance for the retreat center. Make arrangements with the church treasurer for paying the retreat center.

Clergy person as resource. This can be a difficult and confusing role. Retreat committees can vacillate between letting you run the whole program or saying that you don't have to work at all on this retreat, that you can come along and just have fun. Neither option is viable. You can't, and should not, run it all; neither is it wise or possible to completely shed your pastoral role on a retreat. People expect to see you and to relate to you as the minister at this church event.

We have found that the most helpful role is to lead the parts of the retreat which have to do with spiritual growth and worship. A late-night communion, an evening vesper service, Sunday morning worship, or even a time for guided prayer and meditation are all wonderful opportunities for the clergy person to be creative, to be visible, and to assume limited responsibilities.

During the planning process, your role is to nurture and support the coordinator. You can help the committee keep a wholistic vision of the retreat itself and the needs of the congregation as a whole.

Retreat coordinator. This is obviously a big job. Whether you are a staff person or a volunteer, your primary purpose is to keep an overview of the retreat and of each committee member's work. It is important that you not begin taking on responsibilities in other areas, because you will easily be overtaken by events.

Begin by working with the church officer who will help select the committee. The retreat committee needs to be a group representative of the whole church and a group that you will enjoy working with.

Prepare well for the meetings and have the appropriate background material available for each committee member. Be specific about each person's responsibilities. Develop a list of volunteers for the committee members to call on and divide them so that committee members are not calling the same people for their jobs.

Be a nurturer of committee members, communicating the energy and support they need. If any of them cannot continue with their work, you will see that they are replaced gently and with care.

Once the retreat begins, be sure that the individuals in charge of different program areas are visible and identifiable. Give them big nametags so people know whom to question. Otherwise all questions will come to you, which makes for a long repetitious weekend.

After the retreat, supervise setting a date and place for next year's retreat. Read the evaluations, noting concerns for next year, and save them.

Song leader. This may be a dual role. One of the most important ways for people to gather in community is to sing. A good song leader is the cheerleader for the retreat. Begin by having a good resource for singing. There is nothing more frustrating than trying to get a group together for singing and finding that the group does not know enough songs to sing together.

One of the finest songbooks available is *Songs and Creations* by Yohann Anderson which can be ordered from Songs and Creations P.O. Box 559, San Anselmo, California 94960. At this printing the cost is $6.95 per book. Each book has words and chords to over 750 songs, which include old-time favorites, gospel songs, hymns, folk songs, and current popular songs. There is also a tune book which can be purchased separately for $20.00. Individuals can be encouraged to buy their own books. The cost could be added to every first timer's retreat fee. Or the church could buy enough to have available for events like this.

Another option is for the church to make its own songbook or songsheets. There should be enough so that no more than three people have to share together. It is enough to print the words to the songs; the music itself does not have to be printed.

Set aside times in the retreat schedule for people to sing together. The bonfire time is a natural. Exert leadership in the singing. If you are asking for suggestions, keep some order. Veto unsingable songs and go to the next request. Your leadership is a ministry, and your presence in leading the group communicates the spirit of joy, energy, and commitment.

Settle the people before you start. Do not use singing as a way to get people quiet. Direct by singing yourself; do not direct with your arms. Point out that everyone can sing and welcome all singing.

Have fun with the songs. Speed them up; slow them down. Give a verse to the men, women, or children. Have others hum along. Don't be afraid of the old songs, and make sure there is always a new song to learn. Talk about the songs and find out why people request certain songs.

At some point in every singing period, have your own list of selections ready. Have a purpose and direction for the singing and bring it to a meaningful conclusion. Once a tradition of singing has begun, it will remain one of the most powerful and spiritually energizing elements of the retreat.

Chapter 6

Worship in a Retreat Setting

Worship experiences blend into the all-church retreat to define the spirituality of these occasions. While the whole retreat is an energizing experience, people continually recall vespers, bonfires, communion celebrations, and lakeside worship services as the peak moments in their retreats. Songs and stories are often ideal to use in this setting.

Consider first the bonfire as a setting for worship. Our deepest impulses are stirred by the light of a fire. You may have to ring bells and drag people to activities all day, but just light a fire and everybody of every age gathers round the camp circle. The campfire is a place to move from the fellowship of the day into the spirit of God who bonds us.

Songs and stories are natural ways to worship around the campfire. People get very restless if they sense a sermon coming. Children fuss. Young people whisper. Adults fidget. But as soon as it is clear that the medium is a story, the oldest to the youngest quiet down immediately.

The campfire tale is probably as old as the campfire itself. If you are going to lead evening worship around the campfire, spend time looking for and listening to good stories. If there are good story tellers in your congregation, recruit them. The pastor may be the storyteller. If those are not his or her gifts, find someone who has this gift.

One of our favorite resources for campfire stories is a book called *Wonder and Worship* by James Carroll (Newman Press,

Paramus, NJ 1970). Carroll, a Catholic priest when he wrote these stories, has produced a wonderful collection of tales.

For example, Carroll's story "Legs" is a tale of a boy with a disfigured leg who has a recurring dream of a primeval forest. One night in his dream, he discovers a mysterious figure who heals his leg. When the boy awakens, he finds the healing to be real, but his brother sleeping in the next bed now has the disfigured leg. The rest of the story is a suspenseful search through a dream world to find the mystery figure again and reverse this "cellular transference" as the mystery figure calls it. The story is told unsentimentally, with elements of jealousy and rivalry between two young brothers. Carroll suggests resonating scripture from 1 John 3:1-2, 16-19. John 15:13 also fits well.

Another story, "The Sweet Taste of Childhood" is about waiting for the ice cream man. One day a special ice cream man grants the children a wish, and they choose to have ice cream forever. They develop a kingdom of ice cream where everyone is healthy and happy. But they lose the sense of anticipation that came in waiting for the ice cream truck's bells. The ice cream man returns as a beggar years later. His bells remind the king of what they have lost, "A coming to long for and listen to. Something to yearn for, or better, a wandering man to love" (p. 70).

Another fascinating story collection is Jane Yolen's *Tales of Wonder*, Schocken Books, NY 1983. Her's are more enigmatic than Carroll's, but intriguing enough for campfires.

Everyone has their favorite story collections, whether fairy tales, C. S. Lewis, O. Henry, or Rod Serling. Revisit your favorites prior to retreat preparation and find stories that you are comfortable with and that resonate with biblical themes. Consult any collection of Rabbinic tales for good stories to parallel those of the Bible.

Of course the best stories often come right from the Bible. You can interweave songs and hymns easily with many Bible stories.

The story of Jacob leads easily into many songs that go with it. Just a little background takes us back to Abraham and Sarah and the birth of Isaac. Singing "Rocka My Soul in the Bosom of Abraham" along with the story of Abraham and Sarah enhances the story and song.

Going from Abraham to Isaac to Jacob leads to a sharing of all the trickery and reversal that went on in Jacob's life. Jacob's story of looking for a place to stay, resting his head on the rocks, and dreaming of the ladder to heaven leads obviously to singing "Jacob's Ladder."

Matthew Fox suggests that we complete the image of "Jacob's Ladder," by singing "We are dancing Sarah's circle," repeating that line as we do with Jacob's ladder, ending with "sisters, brothers, all." The second verse is "Every ring gets fuller, fuller. . . ." (Matthew Fox, *A Spirituality Named Compassion,* Winston Press, 1979, p. 36). These words recall Sarah's laughter and sense of promise as an important biblical image.

Angels are a part of the story of Jacob. Singing "All Night, All Day, angels watching over me my Lord" can be a good concluding song for the bonfire.

Another cycle of stories can be told around the saga of Moses and the Exodus. The suspense of whether the Pharaoh would ever let the Israelites go can be built up culminating with singing "Let My People Go." The story of Moses can lead into Joshua entering the promised land. A great way to tell the story of Joshua is with the song "Joshua Fit the Battle of Jericho."

Israel's liberation stories also link with stories of slavery and freedom in American history. It is always worth pointing out that American slaves sang spirituals such as "Swing Low, Sweet Chariot" both to sustain their souls as well as to communicate messages of escape. Just as Jacob leads into angels, so "Swing Low" leads into chariot songs such as "Good News, Chariot's Comin' " as a combination spiritual and liberation song.

The Noah story is a favorite for campfires, and the song "Rise and Shine" is one children love.

Ezekial's story of the dry bones can be told in a participatory way. Find a copy of the song "Dry Bones." Invite various children to be each of the bones. When their bone is called, they rise up and join together until all of the bones are dancing around.

Campfires can be closed with times for quiet prayer and for singing classics like "Kum Ba Yah."

Whether your church tradition is high, low, liturgical, or free, the sharing of the Eucharist on a retreat adds a dimension to both the retreat and the communion experience. On a retreat, communion is suddenly freed from many of the restrictions of Sunday morning in the church building.

In the planning process, explore the different times and settings in which the group might like to experience communion. Follow the natural opportunities and traditions of your group. It may be a way of beginning, a way of ending or both. It may be something to be offered to small groups early in the morning or late at night.

For example, our Friday evening program featured orientation sessions where people got to know each other, programs for the children, and introductions to the theme. One year after all of this was over, a group sat down to sing, informally. Little by little, as people put their children to bed, they gravitated to that circle of singers. Around 11:00 p.m. people said it would feel good to close with some kind of worship and sharing.

From that request we developed a tradition of late night communion on Friday nights. It is clearly understood that everyone is not expected at this communion. In fact, as an all-church retreat grows, it is important to make it clear that some events are for the whole community, while others are for small groups. This Friday night communion was meant to be small.

We gather in a comfortable room, preferably a lodge with a fireplace. We usually sit in a circle on the floor, although chairs also work as long as there is a circle. We light candles which are placed aroung the room and in the middle of the circle. We begin with some quiet songs or music or meditation. A reading or scripture passage is shared that fits with the theme of the weekend. A loaf of bread and a goblet of wine are blessed with the traditional words. Then, as the bread is passed, we ask each person to share a response to a question which connects with the retreat theme.

One year we read from Ecclesiastes, "A time for mourning, a time for dancing." Each person was asked to reflect and share on the mourning and dancing in their lives that year. Another year we read the story of Jesus turning the water into wine and asked people to share their sense of the water (the daily routines) and the wine (the celebrative times) in their lives. Once we read a poem by Adrienne Rich about Marie Curie, observing that in her purification of the power of radiation she also wounded her own body. "She died a famous woman, denying her wounds, Denying that her wounds came from the same source as her power." We asked people to share that year their pain and pleasure, reflecting on the ways their power and wounds might come from the same source. In a retreat on family life we used Isaiah's vision of God hammering swords into plowshares and asked people to share how God might hammer a weapon of hurting in their personal or family life into a tool for healing.

Frederick Buechner says, "The gospel is always bad news before it is good news." (Buechner, *Telling the Truth, the Gospel as Tragedy, Comedy & Fairy Tale,* Harper & Row, 1977, p. 7) All of these questions are simple variations on the theme of bad news and good news, which let people both examine and share something of the gospel in their lives. We are very careful to give people the option of not sharing, of simply passing the bread in silence, if that is more comfortable for them. It is important, however, to begin with several people who do share so that there is some modeling. The first time, it may be wise to set up the circle with some people who are primed to be at the beginning.

As the wine is passed, we often sing something simple like "Kum Ba Yah" or listen to music. In closing we encourage everyone to give everyone else a hug. The setting, in a quiet room, with candles and soft music, the children in bed, and a weekend of discovery ahead makes for a special experience.

Another opportunity for communion would be at a morning setting, before breakfast. Again it is important that this be an optional event, available to those who find this a good time for prayer and meditation. To watch a sunrise, climb a mountain, gather by the lake, or light a fire all add to the experience. These are times for silence and meditation and require a minimum of words and verbal sharing.

Finally, Sunday morning worship might well be the one time when the Lord's Supper is offered in a way to include the entire retreat community, gathering the themes raised by the retreat over the weekend. Retreat leaders can help distribute the elements. Depending upon the size of the group, people might share reflections on their experience of the weekend as they receive the bread and wine.

This can be a joyous celebration, with movement, singing, and opportunities for spontaneity. The nature of sharing will depend to some extent on your tradition. It is our belief that since children are intended to be included as participants in the all-church retreat, they should be able to participate in some way in the communion experience.

As with all the suggestions made here, the specific ways you plan your retreat will reflect the theology and tradition of your church. Most people who reflect upon sharing communion at retreats observe that the event overtook particular theologies or traditions. Details debated at deacons or vestry meetings for Sunday morning worship at home fade into the beauty of the celebration itself at retreat. The discussions of theologians and biblical scholars on the form and function of the Eucharistic meal have their place.

But on the retreat the particularities of our disagreements seem strangely unimportant. Here we sense the multiple possibilities for the communion experience—the presence of the Lord in the breaking of bread and the sharing of wine, the power of that presence to make us one not only with Jesus but with one another; and the mystic power of a meal where we understand, without ever having to say it, what it means to love each other.

SUNDAY MORNING WORSHIP

We recommend that the worship service on Sunday morning be the conclusion of the weekend, the final group gathering before lunch or departure. This service must include everyone, even the children, as it is a summation of the retreat experience. Therefore, it should be short, joyous, and celebrative. If you are able to have the service outside, by a lake or in some beautiful spot, the setting will add to the spirit.

It is good to include lots of singing, some old favorites, and the new songs the group has learned during the weekend. If someone can play the flute or recorder, those instruments do well outdoors and can be used to accompany a prayer or moment of silence.

Again, a story works well instead of a sermon. One special story that we like is called "Heaven" from *Wonder and Worship* by James Carroll. It is a story about two dragonflies and is good to tell outdoors. The dragonflies are sitting on a leaf in a lake; one asks the other if he believes in heaven. Not knowing for sure, they fly off in search of it. They fly past the moon, into dark space, eventually losing consciousness and drifting. Suddenly, they see a beautiful world of color and warmth, a glittering plain with jewel-like sparkles. They land to find themselves back on the leaf in the lake where they began. "Heaven?" one asks. "Yes," replies the other.

Various groups may have something to offer for the worship experience. One of our youth groups traditionally makes a worship center from flowers and natural items which they collect. A group of children may have learned a song or dance; they may have a collage or craft to share with the whole group. Sometimes our young people will write a psalm or a prayer for the worship service.

We always end the worship by forming a circle, holding hands, in a large field which is adjacent to the lake. We sing "They'll Know We Are Christians By Our Love" walking together around the circle.

Chapter 7
An Organizational Design

A copy of an all-church retreat program follows. This schedule shows how an all-church retreat looks when all planning comes together. Each person who attends will receive a booklet with the program printed in it. This booklet saves those interminable announcement times on retreats when discussion leaders try to explain to the larger group what they are going to do. It also forces those discussion leaders to develop a simple purpose statement. The booklet is a significant aid to newcomers, because they can look at it and quickly get a sense of the whole retreat.

FRIDAY EVENING	ADULTS	HIGH SCHOOL	MIDDLE SCHOOL
5:30-7:30	REGISTRA-TION in Building B DECORA-TION of the Chapel	FREE TIME	Help with registration
7:30-8:00	FELLOWSHIP TIME with coffee and snacks in the Chapel	Volleyball Practice	Softball Game
8:00	Babysitters on duty until midnight: Building F: Trish and Susan; Cabin A1: Rubye; Cabin A3&4: Tina; Cabin C2: Anna		
8:00-9:00 ①*	BONFIRE AND SINGING FOR EVERYONE at the Bonfire Circle		
9:30-10:30	** "CREATING COMMU-NITY" in the Chapel	9:30-11:30 "Creating Community" in Building B	9:30-11:00 "Playing Tag: games, symbols, and Communion" in Building D 11:15-In cabins
10:45	COMMUN-ION in the Chapel		
12:00	Babysitters off duty	In cabins	
SATURDAY			
7:20	EARLY MORNING YOGA in the Chapel		
8:00	BREAKFAST in the dining hall		
8:45-9:00	WARM-UPS: Stretching and Back Rubs in the Chapel		

Circled numbers refer to notes on page 51.

4th & 5th GRADES	KINDER-GARTEN 3rd GRADE	PRE-SCHOOL	BABIES & TOD-DLERS
Under parental supervision..............................			
Nametags and snack in Building C	Nametags and snack in Building A	Story and snack in Building E	With parents
Babysitters on duty until midnight.			
Bonfire and Singing....................................			
Board Games in Building C 10:20-In cabins	In cabins	In cabins	In cabins
BREAKFAST			
"Community Gathering" and a craft in Building C	Craft in Building A	Craft and play in Building E	With sitters in Building F

** = activities all adults are asked to attend
PARENTS - Please help your children be on time and wear their nametags.

SATURDAY AFTERNOON	ADULTS	HIGH SCHOOL	MIDDLE SCHOOL
9:00	**INTRODUCTION		
9:30 ②	**KEYNOTE SPEECH: "Releasing the Imprisoned Splendor: An Approach to Community Building"		
9:45-10:30	** ADULT DIS-CUSSION GROUPS Responding to the Speech	Special dis-cussion with the speaker in Building B	"Tag Along After" in Building D
10:45	PARENTS, please pick up your children in . . .		
11:00	FREE TIME Waterfront open; lifeguard on duty Canoes reserved for elementary-aged children accompanied by an adult Fun Run—meet on the Chapel porch Challenge Volleyball game between high school group and young adults		
12:00	LUNCH in the dining hall—1st seating for those		
12:15	LUNCH in the dining hall—2nd seating for those		
1:00-2:00		"Community Building" in Building B	Canoeing and waterfront activities
2:00-3:00		Talent Show Rehearsal in Building B	Talent Show Rehearsal in Building D
1:15-2:45	ADULT WORKSHOP GROUPS: a) "Transitions"—meet in Unit C, Cabin 1— What is your pattern for dealing with transitions in your own life? How can you be ready for the next one or clarify the one you are in? b) "Unpacking Love: 1st Corinthians 13"—in Unit B, Cabin 2—St. Paul's classic passage on love can continually surprise us with its timelessness and its capacity to make		

4th & 5th GRADES	KINDER-GARTEN 3rd GRADE	PRE-SCHOOL	BABIES & TOD-DLERS
Soccer Game	Kickball Game	Games and a story	With sitters in Building F
Parents pick up in Building C	Parents pick up in Building A	Parents pick up in Building E	Parents pick up in Building F
FREE TIME			

with small children.

who do not have small children.

4th & 5th GRADES	KINDER-GARTEN 3rd GRADE	PRE-SCHOOL	BABIES & TOD-DLERS
Talent Show Act Preparation in Building C	Quiet activities in Building A	Rest time - to music and stories in Building E	With baby-sitters in Building F
Waterfront Games and Activities	Scavenger Hunt	Nature Walk	With baby-sitters in Building F

** = activities all adults are asked to attend
PARENTS - Please help your children be on time and wear their nametags.

SATURDAY AFTERNOON EVENING	ADULTS	HIGH SCHOOL	MIDDLE SCHOOL
1:15-2:45	ADULT WORKSHOP GROUPS: (continued) us step back from our hustle-bustle world. Come reflect and discuss.		
③	c) "Your Home as a Creative Community: A Time for Reflection as Partners" (repeated identically on Sunday morning)—in Chapel. This seminar will explore our past, present and future homes through visualization, collages, and structured reflection. Open to married couples, married persons and singles; come with a partner.		
3:00	PARENTS, please pick up your children		
3:00-6:00 ④	FREE TIME, to do whatever you wish. 3:00-5:00—Waterfront open with lifeguard; 3:00-4:00—Canoes reserved for 4:00-5:00—Anyone can use canoes; 3:30-5:00—Softball game for adults, young people, 3:30-5:00—Volleyball games on the volleyball 4:00-5:30—The movie, "Never Cry Wolf," in 4:45-5:45—Poetry Reading. "A poem is the		
6:00	DINNER in the Dining Hall—bring a candle.		
6:15	DINNER in the Dining Hall—bring a candle.		
7:00-8:15	FREE TIME. Some groups may wish to rehearse and get ready for the Talent Show.		
8:00	Babysitters on duty until midnight.		
8:15 ⑤	**Talent Show in main room.		
	Afterwards, Snack for adults Folk Dancing Singing	Snack & Movie in Building B	Snack & Movie in Building D 11:15—in cabins
12:00	Babysitters off duty	In cabins	

4th & 5th GRADES	KINDER-GARTEN 3rd GRADE	PRE-SCHOOL	BABIES & TODDLERS
Parents pick up in Building C	Parents pick up in Building A	Parents pick up in Building E	Parents pick up in Building F

children under 14 must have an adult supervisor.
preschoolers accompanied by an adult.
children under 14 must be accompanied by an adult.
and older children.
court.
Building C.
shortest way between two hearts."—in Building A.

First seating for those with small children.

Second seating for those who do not have small children.

In cabins	In cabins	In cabins	In cabins
	Parental discretion	In cabins	In cabins

** = activities all adults are asked to attend
PARENTS - Please help your children be on time and wear their nametags.

SUNDAY MORNING	ADULTS	HIGH SCHOOL	MIDDLE SCHOOL
SUNDAY			
7:20	EARLY MORNING MEDITATION		
8:00	BREAKFAST in the dining hall		
8:45-9:45 ⑥		Canoeing & Waterfront Activities	"Tag Teams" sharing from the weekend
9:45-10:45		Canoeing & Waterfront Activities	Volleyball Game
9:00-10:30	ADULT WORKSHOP GROUPS:		

9:00-10:30 ADULT WORKSHOP GROUPS:
a) "Dealing with Difficult People"—meet at Unit C Cabin 1. In all of our comunities (work, family, social groups, and church), there are people with whom we have difficulty relating? How do we cope? In what ways can we improve or survive with those relationships?
b) "Dreams"—meet in Unit C, Cabin 2. A gestalt approach towards understanding dreams.
c) "Faith and Coping"—meet in Unit B, Cabin 3. A sharing of ideas and experiences of the role of faith in successful, healthful living.
d) "Your Home as a Creative Community"—a repeat from Saturday afternoon.

10:45   PARENTS, please pick up your children . . . .

11:00   **WORSHIP SERVICE by the lake

12:00   ⑦   LUNCH in the dining hall. A completed
1:00-2:00   Waterfront open with lifeguard.
2:30   CAMPGROUND CLOSES.

4th & 5th GRADES	KINDER-GARTEN 3rd GRADE	PRE-SCHOOL	BABIES & TOD-DLERS
Collages about Com-munity in Building C	Craft in Building A	Stories and games in Building E	With baby-sitters in Building F
Scavenger Hunt	Relay Races	A walk to a secret place	With baby-sitters in Building F
Parents pick up in Building C	Parents pick up in Building A	Parents pick up in Building E	With baby-sitters in Building F
Worship Service			With baby-sitters in Building F

evaluation form is your ticket to lunch.

** = activities all adults are asked to attend
PARENTS - Please help your children be on time and wear their nametags.

Sample Evaluation Questions for Adults

1) What did you really enjoy or find valuable at this retreat?

2) What do you like about these camp facilities? What suggestions would you give to the camp management for improvement?

3) Which adult workshops did you attend? What did you enjoy about the workshops? What suggestions do you have for next year?

4) Worship/spiritual nurture. What did you find meaningful or helpful? What suggestions do you have for next year?

5) If you have children, please comment on what worked well for your children in terms of child care and activities. Any suggestions?

6) What benefits, learning, or personal plusses will you be taking home from this weekend?

7) Comments on any other parts of the retreat not already covered.

Sample Evaluation Questions for Children and Young People

Please circle one: high-schooler   middle-schooler
    4th or 5th grader   K - 3rd grader   pre-schooler

1) What did you really like at this retreat?

2) What do you like about the camp itself? What suggestions would you give to the camp for things to improve?

3) Think about the activities which were just for your age group. Which ones were really good—you had fun or learned something or thought were important? What suggestions do you have for your group for next year's retreat?

4) How did it benefit you to come on this retreat?

⑧

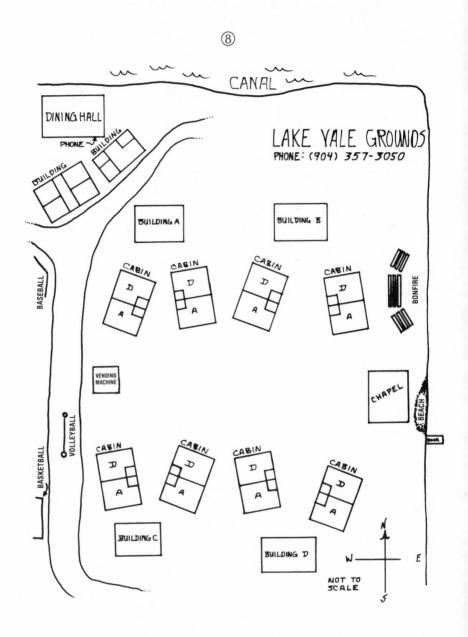

The numbers below refer to the corresponding numbers on the schedule.

1. Friday night is a time for gradual gathering. People leave from work at different times, and the most typical mistake is to plan orientation before the whole group has arrived. Most of the early activities need to be ones which people can join in as they arrive and get settled. This particular year, the bonfire was the major gathering event.

2. The format this year used a keynote speech for the adults. If a variety of discussions are planned, they should be listed with purpose statements and locations. Note that there is a fifteen-minute period following the end of adult discussion groups before children are to be picked up. Without this extra time, children either were loose before the parents arrived or the people supervising the children ran out of things to do while waiting for the parents to come.

3. Note Group C in the afternoon, "Your Home as a Creative Community: A Time for Reflecting as Partners." This group is repeated identically on Sunday morning, so that, at no point, is the whole retreat community split into groups as couples or singles. It also gives couples a choice of when to attend this group if there are other groups they wish to attend or if one of the partners is helping with children's activities at this time. Finally, this keeps this popular group from getting too large. We have found that it is important to have groups for couples and at the same time be very sensitive to the fact that not everyone is in a couple.

4. Later Saturday afternoon is a time for free time and relaxing activities. The events listed are suggested opportunities more than organized groups.

5. Saturday evening can be organized in a variety of ways. Sometimes we have a bonfire vesper experience early in the evening. This year it was decided to hold the bonfire and singing on Friday night; there was folk dancing after the talent show.

A few words about a talent show, a wonderful group building opportunity which can easily go sour. When it is good, individual acts are minimized. Children, young people, and adults do group skits, songs, dances, etc. When it is bad, there is an endless parade of piano solos. Some individual acts aren't bad. They just have to be kept in balance with group activities.

When it is good, the humor involved does not attack others. When it is bad, it slips into the tradition of individuals and groups cutting down each other. Roasting counselors may be fair play in young people's summer camps, but in an all-church retreat, groups need to be careful with satire. It is appropriate for whoever is organizing the talent show to emphasize that acts should have a PG or G rating and not include putdowns.

6. Note again the activities for young people start fifteen minutes before adult discussion groups. This way children can be settled in and adults have time to get to their groups. At 11:00, everyone gathers again for worship and communion, children and adults.

7. The "no evaluation form, no lunch" policy has helped to get feedback on the retreat. A simple evaluation form is important. The advantage of doing it at this time is that there is obviously a high rate of return on evaluations. The disadvantage is that the retreat experience is perhaps too fresh in people's minds for them to offer a significant perspective. It might be advisable to have a follow-up evaluation a week or two later as well. Compile the evaluation results and keep them for next year's planning.

8. No retreat booklet should be without a map. Newcomers can use it for immediate orientation. Even retreat veterans will constantly ask "Where is Building C?" without it. Double check to be sure that the buildings have the same letters or numbers as your map.

A rain plan is an important part of retreat preparation. Rain at any point on this type of weekend can be an annoyance or a real disaster, depending on the facilities and on whether or not you have a rain plan. Encourage people to bring board games. Bring along a VCR with a TV and a few movies for various age groups. The recreation leader should be prepared with some new games, activities which can include many age groups, can be played indoors, and are basically group building.

Another possibility for a rainy afternoon is a do-it-yourself carnival. Everyone returns to their cabins. Each cabin group invents a carnival activity out of what they have with them. They organize and set up this activity in the rec-hall for the whole group. Sponge toss, age guessing, puppet shows, fortune-telling, a fish pond are all possibilities for an afternoon's rain activities.

Chapter 8
Additional Ideas for Themes and Activities

T he previous chapter highlighted a retreat on the theme of "Creating Community." Three additional all-church retreats are featured in this chapter.

"A Rainbow of Diversity: Family Lifestyles"

The picture of the "family that prays together" on the "attend the church or synagogue of your choice" billboards is no longer the norm in American family life. The theme "A Rainbow of Diversity: Family Lifestyles" addresses the difference in family styles while affirming that, in one way or another, we all live in families. It is important in the publicity for this kind of retreat to stress that all of us, whether young or old, married or single, grew up in families and live connected to families in some way. The retreat theme, interpreted in this way, can appeal to everyone.

A key element in the opening of this theme is a "Family Tree" exercise which is included on the next page. Participants are invited to sit in their family groups. Singles may form small groups for collaboration. Family groups are asked to draw a symbolic family tree. The result is a picture of the elements which define a family. An opportunity for sharing is given, and the finished pictures are placed around the building or room. This is an excellent exercise for different ages to share. It helps people explore their family units, giving everyone a way to start thinking about the theme.

Symbolic Family Tree

Think about your family and imagine it as a tree. What kind of tree would best represent your family? Draw that tree.

What kind of soil does your family grow in? Draw the ground around the tree, adding grass or rocks or whatever seems appropriate.

What kind of roots does your family have? Are they long and solid, or short? Are there interruptions in the roots? You may want to draw symbols along the roots to represent different parts of your family's heritage.

Now look at the branches of the tree. Draw one special branch for each family member and put symbols that represent that person along the branch.

NOTE: This exercise works very well for family members to do together, so that each family produces a picture of the tree with all its parts. Several families can then get together afterwards and explain their trees to each other.

If there are singles present, each single should draw his/her own family tree, and then they can get together in a small group to share them.

Supplies needed: One large piece of paper per family or single unit and crayons.

A retreat on this theme may benefit from a resource person familiar with current data on the changing family scene. Most denominations are deeply concerned with this issue and are glad to send a facilitator to meet with local congregations which are considering family life issues.

Adult discussion groups and workshops are good for a family theme. Some suggestions are:

a) "A Third-Quarter Game Plan: Transitions in the Second Half of Life." An important part of middle years is to identify upcoming life transitions. Our goal is to discuss these transitions, to offer connections with each other, and to look at the great psychological and spiritual growth which can occur at this time of life.

b) "Breaking Even—A Financial Success Story of the '80s." Risky and conservative financial strategies will be presented; discussion will range from economic theory to reality.

c) "Ready or Not, Here I Come: Breaking Away." Finding fulfillment and joy often means breaking away from established, predictable patterns. This experience is often accompanied by conflict and confusion. We'll explore these feelings and look at ways to bring a sense of calm to them. This seminar is especially intended for those in their 20's.

d) "Who Cleans the Toilet? Finding a New Balance in Household Roles." Any change in out-of-the-home vocational activities or in family structure can force revision of the in-the-home responsibilities for individual family members. Ways of modifying these roles will be shared and considered.

e) "The Quality of Intimacy."

Session A–Attend with a partner. Focusing on couples, time is provided to think about and discuss intimacy within the relationship. There will be limited sharing by the entire group and small same-sex groups; mostly couples will explore issues of their own connections and their own sexual interaction.

Session B–Attend individually. By interacting in enjoyable and personal ways, we will take a close look at the walls most people build to keep themselves safe and to restrict intimacy. Large and small group discussions and other activities will help each person better understand his/her patterns of making contact with others.

f) "Living With Less: Economic Alternatives." In these times of increasing financial constrictions, many people have less money, time and/or land than they think they will need. Methods will be explored which help us live within limits that society, our personal situation, or the natural environment impose.

g) "Creating New Traditions, Patterns, and Rituals for Fun." An uncle once decided to play classical music during dinner; a couple decided that breakfast out was a good time to make connections. What can we create and enable in our families?

h) "Inventing Families." We will discuss ways for singles, for people without children, for people with family living far away, to create the family roles and members that they need.

i) "Faith and Families." We will consider the role our faith plays in our family life as well as how we can impart our beliefs and values to our children.

An exercise for middle or high school age, which has been done by many groups, fits well with this theme. Each young person is given an egg which has been hollowed out. They name their egg, decorate it to look like a baby, and treat it as if it were their child for the weekend. Every time they want to swim, play or participate in an active event, they have to get a babysitter for their egg. The eggs are meant to suggest the kind of responsibility involved in caring for a child. The message comes across loud and strong as perhaps only 10-20% of the eggs survive the weekend. The rest may be lost, cracked or even dumped in the garbage by mistake with a lunch tray.

Elementary children can have a variety of family theme activities. They might make a collage about their family. They could take a nature walk and learn about families of animals or plants. They could learn songs about families and read stories about families. There are many possibilities.

Another exercise for the whole community is a meal time simulation in which everyone changes family roles. People are asked not to sit with members of their own family. Then individuals at each table are randomly given a family role to play out. The oldest person might be designated as the two-year-old. A third grader might be the father. A teenager might be a visiting aunt. Then let the meal progress. Warning: while some people have a wonderful time with this role playing, other people hate it!

Using a family theme for an all-church retreat can be a powerful experience. The key is in recognizing the variety of family styles and in always including all those varieties in theme and activity planning.

"R & R"

One year, when the committee first gathered to plan for the retreat, the committee members expressed needs and goals as relaxation, rest, fun, and a change from daily routine. We tried to find an intellectual, spiritual, or philosophical theme that year, but nothing fit. Finally, someone looked at all those needs and said, "I think what we all really want is a weekend of 'R & R.' " That quickly became the theme of the retreat. It accurately reflected both the lives of the people and the feeling in the congregation at that time.

As we planned the weekend itself, we kept the goals of rest and relaxation that year. We tried to simplify the jobs for the weekend; we tried to create a low-key, relaxing atmosphere. We also concentrated on having fun as a real means of respite.

We decided that with the theme of "R & R" we should title each retreat event with words that began with the letter R. The committee itself had a great time thinking up the titles. People had fun just reading the retreat program, and it set a tone of rest and fun for the whole event.

Our adult discussion groups for that retreat were:

a) "Relating to Children: Parenting."
>   Session A–focus on middle-school and high-school children, accentuating the positive as well as reducing the negative aspects of the parent-child relationship.
>   Session B–focus on elementary-school and preschool children, as above.

b) "Renewing Your Ties." Attend with spouse or partner. Does your relationship need Renewing, Resolving, Reminding, Refreshing, Releasing, Rejuvenating, Romance? This workshop will focus on getting in touch with each other and with your relationship.

c) "Revisioning Faith: Meditation." Relaxation and meditation techniques will be taught using body and mind for relaxation and a sense of well being.

d) "Reducing Stress." Participants will take the Anxiety Management Skills Inventory to assess their stress management skills in nine different areas. Inventories will be scored during the workshop and suggestions for improving stress and anxiety management will be offered.

e) "Rising Stars." A semi-structured group experience which allows for exploration of role-taking in social interactions. Especially designed for those persons ages 18 to 32.

f) "Rehabilitate Your Body: All You've Ever Wanted to Know about Exercise." Learn about the benefits, what actually happens to your body, when you exercise.

g) "Recreational Stitchery." Bring your handwork; sit and stitch.

h) "Revisioning Faith: Roads to Redemption." Taking a look at Exodus 6:6-7 and Deuteronomy 26:5-6, we will rediscover the core liberation story of the Old Testament. Through group sharing and guided experimential exercises, we will discuss the meaning of this tradition in our individual lives.

i) "Redirections: People in Transition." This workshop will be an opportunity to explore and discuss the many transitions we go through in our lifetime and to look at ways to maximize the potential for growth in these situations.

Children's activities had equally good titles: "Reflecting on Relationships"; "Rebounding Soccer"; "Real Games"; "Relaxing Crafts"; "Reviving Waterfront"; "Restful Films and Stories"; "Rousing Sing-a-long"; "Reaching into the Reservoir of our Faith"; "Retelling Bible Stories"; and "Recreational Kickball."

This particular retreat came after one which had been excellent, yet highly structured and challenging. It is good to remember to vary the emotional tone as well as content of retreats. If the retreat is to become a yearly event, then each one can have a very different flavor and schedule.

"The Balancing Act: Living with Competing Demands"

This theme grew out of the first meeting of a retreat committee when each committee member was asked to introduce him/herself and comment on a current sense of what his/her life was like. The commonality which surfaced from that sharing was a focus on competing demands and the difficulty of balancing all the roles and activities which each person wanted to do. It was an excellent theme; it generated lots of good ideas. One member of the group drew a picture of a clown on a sagging tightrope wobbling back and forth with a striped umbrella over his head. It was a good symbol for the way life often feels.

The adult discussion groups for this theme were:

a) "Balancing Expectations and Reality in Marriage." Expecting too much from a marriage leads to anger and stress; expecting too little lets relationships wither and die. This experience will be an opportunity for partners to share expectations openly and balance them with reality in such a way that they produce the positive feelings of growing love.

b) "Can I Take a Bubble Bath While D.C.'s Burning?" This year, political campaigns and social issues beckon, and many of us will respond by giving a significant amount of time and energy. The trick is being effectively involved while maintaining a healthy self. In this workshop, each person will share past success/failure in this balancing act.

c) "Environment I: Growth vs. Conservation." A discussion of the factors involved in the continuing controversy about balancing growth and conservation in our state.

d) "The Time Management Blues." We will use a handout listing 30 popular methods to save or manage time. Participants will identify and discuss those methods most likely to promote personal growth.

e) "Career and Family: Balancing from a Woman's Perspective." (for men and women) How do we make our decisions about what we want to be when we grow up? What kinds of concerns do we deal with when the demands of our jobs conflict with the rest of our lives?

f) "Massage: The Art of Balance Through Touch." Come with a partner to learn massage.

g) "Career and Family: Balancing from a Man's Perspective." (open to men and women) There have been significant changes in the areas of career pursuit and family roles during the past fifteen years. We will explore both ends of the spectrum and the balance that exists between them.

h) "Environment II: Comfort vs. Responsibility." A roundtable discussion to examine the consequences of daily living on the environment. We will address ways to balance our comforts with our environmental responsibilities.

i) "The Wellness Movement and Personal Growth." This workshop will be an opportunity to learn the specific aspects of living in a whole, healthful way.

j) "Commitment: Why Get out of the Bathtub?" What motivates me to get involved? Did you ever wonder "What could I have possibly been thinking of when I agreed to do that?" A chance to look at our commitments.

k) "Learning How To Juggle." Real tennis balls and things like that.

All of these themes and workshop suggestions are meant to be the background for generating your own ideas. A theme is an umbrella for the retreat, under which are opportunities for spiritual growth, community building, relaxation, and challenge.

Chapter 9
The Schedule

Y ou will begin with a basic outline from the retreat center or camp with their concerns: when you can arrive, when meals are served, when their lifeguard is available, and when you have to leave. Write all of this down and then begin to fill in around these times.

Before you start adding individual activities, it is good to consider the flow of the weekend. On the first day or night, you should have a gathering event, something which everyone can attend and which, by its nature, helps people feel connected. (You will want to have another gathering event at the end of the weekend.) Then you can schedule interest-oriented events throughout the next time periods. We recommend alternating more serious activities with recreational activities. By Saturday afternoon at 2 or 3 o'clock, no matter how wonderful your program is, people will fade out. This is a good opportunity to schedule free time. You should also offer worship/ spiritual opportunities of various kinds at different times throughout the weekend.

One common mistake on first retreats is not to allow enough time between events. It takes a large group about twenty to thirty minutes to move from one event to another. Thus, if your check-in time ends at 7:30, your gathering event could begin at 8:00. Allow at least forty-five minutes for breakfast and an hour for lunch and dinner. Begin adult activities fifteen minutes after the children's activities start, giving parents a chance to deliver and settle their children and then arrive at their own events. End adult activities fifteen minutes before the children's event.

Specify some of the events that you want eveyone to attend, and then let other events be optional. You do not want people to feel overprogrammed or overscheduled. The person who really needs time to be alone by the lake will resent feeling pressured to be at every adult workshop, but will appreciate some direction as to when his/her presence is needed.

Underscheduling is an equal pitfall. Some people are very comfortable with a loose, free-floating weekend in which they make their own program. For others, that feels like being lost, and their anxiety level goes way up. By providing a structure, with options for dropping out, you can meet the needs of both personality types.

When your committee has finished planning its retreat, schedule one more meeting two weeks after the retreat which need not involve the whole committee. Include enough key committee members to process the evaluations and make the initial plans for next year.

Retreat centers must be reserved a year in advance, so the primary decision of this group will be when and where to hold next year's retreat. If there is a strong consensus to move to a new site, or if the last site is not available, this group becomes the first explorers for next year's location.

While programs are fresh in everyone's mind, collate a summary of recommendations for next year. Gather special evaluations from committee members not participating in this meeting and group leaders. Set a date for next year. Make a poster. Get it on the church calendar. Next year's retreat is already begun.

Summary Reflections

After looking at all these details, it is important to step back and reconsider the larger picture of the all-church retreat. It is not necessary to follow every instruction or include every element offered here. The simple fact of getting members of your congregation of various ages away together on a retreat has its own power, drawing strength from the spirit which flows through the church itself and returning new vitality and fellowship to the church. Keep this priority in mind. Do not use the all-church retreat for church planning or officer training. Those are good agendas for other occasions. The surest way to put a damper on the unique nature of this event is to use it to work on the problems of the church. Rather the all-church retreat should be a celebration of and consolidation of community.

Be patient with the process of planning and building the all-church retreat. Like all spiritual journeys, the all-church retreat generally begins rather clumsily. After you have done it the first time, there will be revisions and changes you will want to make for the second retreat. We have done thirteen all-church retreats, and we make changes every year. There is no such thing as a perfect retreat. Our motto is, "We're always making it better." Something always goes wrong, or on the way home you think of something that would have made a particular event better.

Offer adventure and fun to the participants, not perfection. Our second slogan is "Don't expect Disneyworld." This is always a developmental journey.

Underlying all our advice and helpful hints in fine-tuning the retreat process is the assumption that the most important step is the first leap of faith. In setting out together as a church we trust in God to embrace the ensuing retreat with the arms of grace. "Underneath all are the everlasting arms," says the book of Deuteronomy. By trusting in God we experience those arms, gently cradling us and urging us on.

Section II
Youth-Group Retreats

Introduction

Youth groups are the natural constituents for retreats. Young people enjoy being together. They are happy to get away from home, and they are at an ideal developmental time for spiritual growth. For these reasons, youth-group retreats are the easiest of all to organize.

However, for other reasons, they are full of pitfalls which cause difficulties for anyone trying to facilitate such a retreat. Edwin Friedman points out in his book *Generation to Generation* (Guilford Press, New York, 1985), people tend to carry the dynamics of their nuclear families into the family settings of the church. All the unresolved issues of a teenager's family may easily be acted out in resistance to planning and attending a youth-group retreat. Parents who had negative emotional experiences in their own youth-group retreats, or who resent the fun teenagers might have on such a retreat, or who are just at odds with their teenager, may erect all kinds of roadblocks to prevent this retreat from happening or to prevent their child from attending. Young people in conflict with authority at home may bring that conflict into the retreat experience. Adult leaders with unfinished business from their adolescence may find themselves reliving their own uncertainties when they work with adolescents.

Lest all of this sounds too overwhelming, remember that the benefits usually outweigh the costs with youth-group retreats. It is often enough simply to be aware of the elements of family systems which typically bleed into church events such as a youth group retreat. When obstacles arise in developing youth-group retreats, it is as important to explore the family systems issues as the planning process itself.

This section of *The Retreat Handbook* explores the dynamics of planning and carrying out youth-group retreats. Our thesis is that youth groups are part of the family system that is the church, and activities for youth-group retreats must relate to that system. In this section we will discuss ways to uncover the special characteristics of each youth group, especially as these characteristics relate to small, middle-size, and large youth groups.

We will look at how these retreats can reflect the particular developmental stages and marker times of adolescents. We will then focus on planning high-school retreats, first in general and then in offering some specific themes and programs.

The emphasis in all these retreats will be making them developmentally appropriate for their age group and integrating the youth-group experience into the setting of the church and the young person's family. We emphasize this connection so strongly since adolescents are beginning to establish their independence and the easiest way to bond them as a group is to set them up against a common enemy. Both the church and the young person's parents make convenient targets. It is easy for youth-group leaders to develop a quick bond with a youth group by working against the church and the young peoples' parents. We believe that this situation should be avoided at all costs. It is a quick-fix approach to youth leadership, destructive of the goals of growth and healthy development which youth groups need to nurture. Instead, the youth-group retreat should be a healthy blend of independent exploration that includes the support and encouragement of the young person's church and family of origin.

Chapter 10
Sizing Up Your Youth Group

E ach youth group is unique, but within your own uniqueness are shared characteristics. Unfortunately, most resource material for youth groups seems to be written for a large youth group with full-time professional staff. Most churches, however, are small churches. Therefore, most youth groups struggle with size. The first affirmation of the special nature of your youth group is its size. Small, middle, and large youth groups all have special gifts.

The Small Youth Group

The small youth group has six to twelve attending members. It may be a new group starting up, an old group dwindling, or the maximum size one could expect given the size of the church. In each case planning sessions will probably include someone saying, "Hey, we've got to get more people interested in coming."

Right from the start, the adult leadership should see how this comment fits into the larger system of the church. If this is a small church with potential for growth, such excitement reflects the overall attitude of the church. If it is a small church in a community with a limited number of young people to draw from, such a statement may be one of frustration. If it is a dwindling church with a youth group losing members, it may be a cry for help, a sign of discouragement or depression.

As a leader you need to fit this concern for growth into the larger context of the church. The reality for all groups is that they *can* grow. Affirm that such growth is good and will come, but that for the moment the group is fine as it is. The group members who are here now are valuable and need to be told that. The greatest difficulty members of a small group have is in feeling that there is something wrong with them for being there and that a good group is a big group. The first round of activities planned for such a group should demonstate that small is beautiful.

Take time exploring the gifts of each member. Let each member share his or her favorite activities or favorite songs, the hobbies that bring them joy, what they do best of all. Let them see how important they are in a small group and then weave their joys into events that communicate the ways everyone's gifts can be celebrated in a small group.

At the same time it is probably important for the adult leadership to have a long-term agenda for growth. A group can survive and prosper with 10-12 members. Fewer than that is truly difficult.

The future growth can come in a number of ways. First, develop strong programs for younger children. It is difficult for teenagers to break into existing peer groups. Good elementary programs, however, are the feeder systems for growing youth groups. It is easier to involve friends and newcomers in younger age groups. If the high-school group is weak, build a strong middle-school group. If the middle-school group is struggling, develop a good elementary program.

Second, look at the potential list of young people on your church roster. Inactive young people may be just as difficult to involve as inactive adults. This is not, as the missionaries say, a fruitful field for harvest. It should, however, be checked.

Third, consider whether you want your people to invite friends to the group. The best time to do this is for special events such as swimming parties, short trips, or movies. Sometimes friends offer just the spark a group needs. Other times they can divide an already disengaged group. If friends are going to be included on a retreat, plan some activities into the beginning of your program which will help integrate the friends into the group.

Many churches try to combine ages with small youth groups. Occasionally, this approach can work as a temporary solution, but it is seldom a long-term solution to the problem of growth. We do not recommend inviting older elementary to be part of a small junior high or middle-school group. Neither is it good to combine junior- and senior-high groups. The developmental age categories of a school system are important markers in growing up. Combinations may excite the younger group momentarily, but eventually the members of the older group will drop out . There is simply too much difference in the needs and experiences of a 7th-grader and a 12th-grader.

The primary message here is to walk that razor's edge of affirming the gifts of a small group while gently enabling it to grow enough to sustain itself. Once you have identified your small group and affirmed it as such, a retreat is an excellent way to strengthen the community of that group. Begin your planning by affirming all the interesting things a small group can do which might be too cumbersome for a large group. For example, a small group can all travel together in one van. They can go quite a distance with minimal difficulty. They can take a camping trip, use a church member's summer house at a lake, beach, or mountain. They might go to a resort in an off-season or rent a condominium. Often a small group can all sleep in the same room (with adults present of course!). Such possibilities develop excitement and are preferable to reserving one small cabin at a denominational conference center where your group will be surrounded by large groups, which just make them feel inferior.

Do not overwhelm the small youth group with adults. If your church is deeply committed to developing or revitalizing the youth program and has signed on six or eight youth advisors, don't let the advisors outnumber the young people at meetings. Use them as resource people, drivers, food buyers. But do not have six adults staring at six young people in a planning meeting.

Realize that a small group cannot sustain the same length of discussion as a larger group. Times of serious exploration can be shorter than in a larger group where it takes longer to develop trust and hear everyone's perspective. Therefore you have more time for games and free time in a small group.

Again, realize that it will be difficult for a small group to organize itself into free-time activities. You may have to demonstrate the advantages of this size. Rework traditional sports to be compatible with your youth group. For example, volleyball can be played indoors using a balloon and having three people on a side. Outdoors you can play one-bounce volleyball. Softball can be played with just one base, positioned behind the pitcher's mound. Every hit ball is fair, and every baserunner has to run on every hit ball. Virtually every sport can be set up to be played by a small number of players. Young people in a small group all get to be stars, an experience everyone should have but which does not come for everyone in a large group.

The same principle applies to spiritual explorations, personal sharings, and worship. Make these affirming, simple, positive experiences, and the small group can have a wonderful time.

Just as a small church is organically different from a large church, so a small youth group is organically different from a large one. Do not try to mimic a large group. And while everyone in a community notices and applauds the large youth-group ventures run in large churches with professional staff, remember that it is more difficult to run a youth program in a small church where there are few teenagers, fewer resources, and no paid help. Give yourself and your volunteers lots of pats on the back because it is not an easy job. Your group may be small, but your impact on your young people is immeasurable.

The Middle-Size Youth Group

Like the middle-size church, the middle-size youth group is by its very nature in transition. What is happening in the church of the middle-size youth group? Is your church growing, declining, at a plateau? Does the size of the youth group reflect the size of your church? A middle-size youth group has 12-25 attending members. A middle-size church has 125-200 in attendance on Sunday morning.

Like the church, the middle-size youth group is probably understaffed. Middle-size youth groups tend to sandwich their leadership between other responsibilities. Either a single clergy person, a volunteer, or an associate pastor with many other responsibilities has this job.

Again, the first step in dealing with a middle-size group is to affirm it. If the group has grown from a small group, that is usually exciting. But at the same time, there are growing pains. Some members remember when there were less than a dozen people in attendance, and they felt much more special. The youth budget has probably not caught up with the growth of the group, so resources are slim. If the church membership and youth membership are in decline, this may mean budget and staff cutbacks which leave everyone with a free floating sense of depression.

Beware of the temptation to covet the neighboring large church with its budget, bus, and full-time staff! Actually, a youth group of 12-25 is a wonderful size. There are enough people so that members can feel like they are part of a good idea. The group is small enough to remain inclusive of everyone. Growth for a group this size should be comfortable and natural.

Somewhere the leadership needs to find that balance between letting a group stagnate at this size (very easy because it is so comfortable) and overdoing the pressure to grow. Keep nurturing upcoming classes and work to involve younger members in the group.

In planning retreats, two or three adults should be involved. They can help each other with perspective, and when going on a retreat with this size, there should be enough adults so that they can relate to five or six young people each.

The middle-size group still has a lot of flexibility for retreat sites. Again be creative. Every retreat does not have to be at a denominational camp. In fact, the middle-size group may still be too small to fill up conference center facilities by itself. A combination of motel rooms, resort lodges off season, or a member's summer home may still be possible for the middle-size group.

Another option for the middle-size group, since funds are often a problem, is using the church. Young people often enjoy staying overnight at the church. It gives them a special sense of ownership of the church as theirs. The church building becomes more of a holy space for them. By staying at the church, you can use many of the resources of your own community for the program. An obvious pitfall is the difficulty in separating the group from everyday activities of the community, but this can be effectively dealt with.

A third way for a middle-size group to find a retreat center is to join with another group of similar size. Two middle-size groups can rent a bus together or reserve an entire conference center and enjoy each other's company without losing the integrity of their own group. Care must be taken in choosing another group with compatible leadership styles and planning expectations.

Remember the key word for middle-size groups is transition. Leadership, size, membership, budget may all be changing at different times. Be alert to the direction your group is moving and plan accordingly. If the group is becoming larger, then it is time to start splitting into subgroups for discussion and planning. If it is getting smaller, then it will be important to consolidate resources and affirm the strengths that can be shared as a single-unit group.

The Large Youth Group

If you have over twenty-five regularly attending members of your youth group, you have a large group. We are not going to make distinctions between the large youth group of say 25-35 members and what might be called the "super group" of 100+ members. In the latter case, you are running a minischool, but some of the same principles suggested here will apply.

The large group is the classic blessing and curse rolled into one. Everyone looks to the large group as the ideal. Many clergy have grown up in large youth groups. The large group has the momentum, the peer-group support, and the sheer strength of numbers to keep it moving in its charted direction. The problem here is that if that is not a healthy direction, it may be difficult to change course. This is why it is important to do good goal setting and organizational design for the large group.

Most likely the leadership will be from a full-time associate pastor or trained youth director. This may well be someone rather young who feels the weight of great expectations laid upon him or her to keep up the high level of programming for the large group. Therefore, the first task for the professional leadership of a large youth group is to build a good support team of other adult leaders. The very large group may find it possible to hire one or two part-time lay staff members. This is generally an excellent idea and relatively inexpensive for the multistaff church.

If the clergy person is under thirty, then it will be important to utilize older adults as part of the leadership team. It is especially important to involve parents of teenagers as background support. Most churches immediately assume that young adults should work with youth. While young church members should be involved with youth, "mature" adults are also a necessary component of the leadership team. The inclusion of older adults guards against the trap of the younger staff and committee members identifying with the youth group over and against the church as a whole. If this happens, then parents of youth-group members become resentful and lose their trust of the group. It is not long before the classic split between the youth group and the adult church develops with the deacons, vestry, or senior pastor laying out a long list of rules for youth programs that ultimately make everyone feel bad and don't really work. We recommend mixing the ages of the adults on the youth-group leadership team, looking for a combination of adults who are in their twenties and those adults who are in their thirties and forties.

It is also politically important to involve adults near the age of the young people's parents. This builds a bond with the parents. It helps in the kinds of decisions that have to be made on retreats about the exceptional requests young people make which you can never quite predict ahead of time. Things like, ''A couple of us are just going to ride into town with David to pick up the medicine for his allergies that he forgot,'' or ''How about letting us go swimming—it's really warm for February.''

On the other hand, if the clergy leadership is in that ''mature'' age range, it is then important to recruit some younger adults to assist for the same reasons listed above except in reverse. There need to be people in touch with the music, social pressures, and styles of youth.

A mixed age group of adult leadership is an important start. It builds trust among parents. It keeps the leadership distinguished from the group. And it keeps the activities of the leaders honest. Youth work can be very seductive.

Next, build a good leadership corps from the young group. Any group planning should include the young people. With the large group, this is essential. Gather your youth representatives carefully so that they do represent the group, can offer leadership, and help with ideas. It is very important to involve the young people in planning, because the large group easily settles into waiting for the adults to entertain them.

Retreats are wonderful experiences for large youth groups. Significant advance planning is important. Since you will probably need a good size retreat center, you may have to reserve the site a year in advance. In looking for a site, do not remain confined to your own denomination for resources. Check with other religious groups, the ''Y,'' or the conference packages offered by resorts and lodges. The larger the group, the more important it will be to have a site where you have control over your whole group.

Utilize your adult support team for help with food, driving, recreational supplies, etc. This is an especially good place to use parents. Youth-group directors easily burn out trying to shop and cook for thirty-six teenagers.

Take along enough adults so that discussion groups and activity groups can be broken down into manageable sizes for sharing. Youth groups typically resist splitting into smaller groups, but it is important that discussions happen in groups of twelve or less so that everyone has a chance to share.

Rules need to be developed by the planning group with a clear understanding of limits set by the adult leadership. These can then be presented and negotiated with the whole group, and changes can be made in areas where the adult leadership feels flexible. It is always better to have these limits and rules worked out ahead of time than to have to backtrack on the retreat itself.

Keep in mind the unique needs of your group and its relationship with your church. If your group needs a sense of its own identity and power, use that identity in your theme and programming. If it needs more connections with the church itself, then work on ways to include the people, themes, and goals of the church in its retreat. There is always the option mentioned for the smaller youth groups of using the church building as a retreat site. Most churches have lots of space, and meeting in the church for an important informal event gives the young people a chance to get to know their own church and community for a special weekend. Off-limits areas must be identified at the start so that no one climbs over the organ pipes in a game of hide and seek.

Activities for a large group should have a mixture of choices for small groups, voluntary interest groups which people can choose to attend or not, and then activities in which everyone is expected to be a part. This is true for recreational, educational, and spiritual activities.

Recreation activities need to give people opportunities to do different kinds of games as well as to gather from time to time in activities for the whole group. "Platooning" teams in soccer or volleyball can involve lots of people. Getting a "moonball" game on a large field can involve everyone.

The larger the group the more important it will be to form special-interest groups which affirm the different gifts of members. Music and arts groups, intramural sports teams, study groups, all can be developed on retreats. And just as important as finding the unique gifts of the different members, is bringing the group together again as a whole.

The key to running a large youth-group retreat is to be a good planner and organizer. Develop a good support team of adults and use the leadership of the youth group. Keep breaking down the group into manageable units, and give those small groups good contact with competent adult leadership. Have a good schedule available at all times. Young people, staff, volunteer adults, and parents should all know exactly what is going on.

With all these components in place, the large youth-group retreat can be one of the most rewarding experiences of the church for both the young people and the adults working with them.

Summary

The programs and suggestions for youth-group retreats offered in the rest of this section can all be adapted to the small, middle, and large youth groups. First, however, each group's special gifts must be affirmed. The small group needs to feel good about itself as it is. Leadership needs to affirm the possibilities this small group has in supporting each member. The middle-size group needs to be aware of the transitions it is in and develop a staffing style to meet those needs. The large group needs to be highly organized and clear about its expectations and directions. Once you are aware of the unique elements of your group, you can then focus on the common characteristics of youth-group retreat planning.

Chapter 11
Key Elements in the Youth-Group Retreat

T he first step in planning a youth-group retreat is gathering a planning team. This team should include adult leaders and youth representatives. With this team, evaluate the needs and concerns of the current youth group.

One method of understanding the group is to consider three basic levels of group process. The first is individual. Here a person explores, within the context of the group, "Who am I? What are my gifts, my strengths, my concerns?" Once the individuals feel secure the next step can be taken, which is group building. Trust is built as members ask "Who are you?" and affirm each other's gifts and positive qualities. Secure in their own gifts and affirmed in trust by each other, they can move to the third level of group function, undertaking such activities as goal setting, mission tasks, and worship planning and leadership. Another way to state this is that every group must progress from "Who am I as a person" to "Who are we together" and then to "What do we want to be and do as a group?"

Usually, when the process of a group breaks down, it signals a need to go back to the previous level of group function. For example, if a group is trying to plan a worship activity and only one person is talking, arguments keep breaking out, or a general sense of impatience arises, it means that the second level of group affirmation has to be revisited. If people cannot affirm each other's gifts, then move back to step one and give people an opportunity to explore their own identity.

Of course the same analysis is true to the planning group. This group, too, may well need to start by letting each member explore his or her individual gifts. Then let the group members affirm each other, enabling each other's strengths to arise.

Positive brainstorming is often a good way to build trust in a planning group. In brainstorming, every idea is welcomed and recorded. Leaders quickly work to include all ideas in umbrella themes and concerns. Right away, individuals find their contributions valued. The group sees individual strengths pooled to become group strengths.

The planning group may see the youth group as a whole to be ready for mission. They can then plan a retreat in which some very sophisticated action plans can be developed. A group which needs to get to know each other could have a retreat where individuals begin to explore who they are. Too often leaders hammer away at a given group level rather than move back to a level in which members can begin to function together.

Once the planning group has gained a sense of its identity and has a sense of where the youth group is functioning, it is time to begin exploring themes for the retreat. These themes should include within them the possibilities for spiritual growth, education, group building, and recreation. The theme will then suggest the kind of site suitable for the retreat.

Here we run into the "Catch-22" of all retreat planning—site selection. Often this needs to be done far in advance of the actual date. However, you can never get a youth group to do serious planning a year in advance. You will just have to learn how to blend the needs of your group with the retreat sites available to you.

In choosing a retreat site, keep these issues in mind. If you are concentrating on group building for your group, you won't want to be where there are other youth groups. If your group is at a high level of development, however, they may benefit from contact with other groups. If your group is ready for a task, you may want a retreat with a strong educational or action plan; in this case you may want to go to a city or religious community where the group will be exposed to new ideas and cultures. If your group needs to have fun, pick a place with good recreational opportunities. We once found a Young Life retreat center that was specifically developing a site attractive to inner city groups. It had Go Karts, horseback riding, a pool, a lake, a series of good athletic fields, and a wonderfully equipped recreation room. If you wanted to do deep spiritual exploration, that would not be the right place. If you wanted social activities, it would be.

With a direction and a site selected, brainstorm the ways to approach your particular goals. Do you want to create a simulation experience for the whole weekend? Will discussion groups be sufficient? Do you need resource people for facilitation and leadership? How much input does the group as a whole want and need?

After the planning group has decided on a theme and found a site, begin to develop a schedule. Balance the fun with serious times. Give ample opportunity for the young people to be on their own. In his book, *The Hurried Child—Growing Up Too Fast, Too Soon* (Addison Wesley, 1981), David Elkind described the ways that young people are pushed, programmed, and directed in many different activities for most of their waking hours. Sports, music lessons, studies, and social events all fill up their schedules. Church youth-group retreats can be just one more pressured place in teenagers' lives, or they can be places where there is time for relaxation, play, and spontaneity.

After the schedule is developed, begin to delegate responsibilities. Youth directors are notorious for trying to do too much themselves. Driving, grocery shopping, and getting supplies can all be done by other adults, including parents, and young people.

Then comes the crucial task of getting clear attendance commitments from the young people. We are back in "Catch-22" again. On the one hand, you may have to plan a date far in advance. As much as possible, get the school schedules for holidays, exams, footfall games, band concerts, SAT's, proms, chorus trips, or any other school or community event which requires their presence. Even with these schedules, it is important to remember that school events are difficult to pin down and are subject to last-minute changes. Pick one or two target dates for the retreat. Once these target dates are identified, have the young people check their calendars and their parents' calendars for conflicts. Then establish whatever plan is reasonable for encouraging the young people to make and keep a commitment to the youth-group retreat. Usually a nonrefundable deposit helps.

When you open your retreat for registration, include a place for parents to sign up to help with food, transportation, or supplies. If you plan to use any of your young people as drivers, it is a good idea to have a place on the registration form where parents can check if they are willing to let their children ride with teenage drivers. Include with the registration a medical release form authorizing medical personnel to treat the child in case of emergency. Included on that form should be information about how the parents can be reached during that weekend. A sample form follows on the facing page.

Keep the parents informed every step of the way. If possible, have a parent or two on the planning committee. If necessary, have a parents' meeting to explain the plans and expectations for the retreat. Get their input about what they want for their young people. Parents are good allies. If they are uncomfortable with what you are doing, they can easily undermine your best attempts.

Explain to parents that grounding young people from youth-group retreats should not be used as punishment for grades or disciplinary problems at home. All young people need time to get away, explore who they are, and experience the small beginnings of adulthood that living with a community other than their family offers. Families have many other prohibitions they can place on their children. Ask parents to restrict TV, a social event, afternoon time with friends, or other activities instead of taking away church youth events.

While this is a time when young people are moving away from their parents developmentally, parents still want to and should be involved in their children's lives. Youth leadership can retain the trust and confidentiality of young people without keeping information from parents unnecessarily. Help the parents by sharing with them your hopes and goals for the young people and continue to solicit their input. With parents involved as a backdrop to the youth program, and young people having active responsibility for what is happening, you will be well-positioned for the retreat itself.

The specific program will determine many of the particular elements of the retreat. There are some general guidelines.

Tom Erney, educational consultant with the Quest National Center, offers these suggestions. First, it is important to provide a structure so that young people know what is expected of them and what to expect of the experience. They should not have to guess what the schedule will be, what their limits are, and what responsibilities they will have. Outline the goals and purposes of the retreat. As the adult leader, you need to be clear about what you want to happen and where you are willing to negotiate. Involve

Registration Form For Youth-Group Overnight

Name _____ Grade _____

Address _____

Phone Number _____ Birthday _____

    I give my child, _____, permission to attend the United Church Youth-Group Retreat, March 6-7, 1986. I authorize the chaperones of that retreat to secure any emergency medical care which may be necessary for my child during that time. I agree to pay in full for such care.

    My insurance policy number is _____ and the insurance company is _____.

    I can be reached during that weekend at the following address and phone number: _____
_____.

_____
Signature

It is ok with me if my child rides in a car driven by one of
    the seniors in the group _____ OR
I would prefer that my child ride in a car with an adult driver
_____.

the young people at this point with setting some of the structure of the retreat so that they have some ownership of the program. The teenagers then do not have to act out to find your limits of leadership. Be up front with your willingness to negotiate up to the point of your limits.

Second, post the ground rules and remind the young people of their importance. These are group norms, established early in the event; they do not evolve as you go along. Then you personalize the atmosphere by creating a sense of safety and security. For instance, one ground rule could be "No put-downs by anyone." You point out that this is different from their normal school environment.

Third, throughout the program have opportunities for personal sharing by going around the circle, asking each young person to share on a topic. Start with simple, nonthreatening topics and move to heavier ones. Always give the young people an opportunity to pass, as individuals, on any topic. There should be an expectation that you are going to push the risk level gently. The leader does this by modeling the sharing and the listening, beginning each round himself or herself.

Fourth, keep a balance between writing and talking. Writing gives young people time to think and the security of reading from a paper. Often there is more participation and less passing if they share after they have written their thoughts. Writing offers a balance between the outer and inner self.

Fifth, use some of the other good resources which young people enjoy. Music, especially their music, is a powerful supplement. Ask a member of the youth group to make a tape of current music which reflects the theme of the retreat and use this music as background for some nonverbal activities. Have them draw from time to time with markers or water colors. Put posters up around the room, with quotes or pictures which relate to the theme or to philosophies about life. Use these posters and pictures as starting points for some discussions. A board or newsprint that can be used as a graffiti wall is fun. Use lots of papers and markers to write down the main points of the discussion. Continue to confirm their contributions by writing down what young people have said.

Sixth, bring each session to some closure. Go around the circle and ask the young people to finish the sentence, "I learned . . ." or "I see that I need to relearn . . . ." Begin the next session by touching on the high points of the last session. You are constantly integrating what has already been said with what you are going to do.

Seventh, Erney concludes, always personalize their learnings. Ask them to give examples where this has happened in their lives. For example, rather than discussing the general principles of racism, ask them when they have experienced prejudice themselves. Remember the 3 R's of discussion: Keep it relevant, real, and right now.

There are other specific retreat issues which are good to address during the planning. The first is bedtime, which can often be a time for young people to push limits. Have your own limits in mind, and then ask the group to come to a consensus about a reasonable time to go to sleep. If the adults decide the bedtime, the young people will argue, no matter how late the adults have decided. If the young people are allowed to make this decision, usually they will be more conservative than you. If they are unreasonable, negotiate. If they want to stay up until 1:00 a.m., and you feel uncomfortable with that, offer a compromise on bed by 12:00 and quiet by 1:00.

Sometimes, if the group is small enough and a room is large enough, it works well to have the whole group sleep together in one room. Obviously the adult leaders are also in the same room. The young people don't have to divide into roommates. They enjoy being together as boys and girls, and they are easier to manage than in any other setting. They can't sneak into each other's rooms. They are already there! Keep a dim light on and you can see exactly what is going on. There is no need to keep checking rooms. But there will have to be a firm time for everyone to be absolutely quiet. Another option for quieting down the quiet time is to bring a VCR and show a movie. Find a video that resonates with the theme. Show it very late when everyone is in his or her sleeping bag and let the young people fall asleep watching it. The key is enabling the young people to stay up late enough that they feel they have had a good time and getting enough sleep to be able to continue the retreat.

Dividing up routine jobs or chores is another task to consider. Pick any procedure that avoids the three possible disasters of a retreat: you don't want to do all the dirty work yourself; you don't want two or three responsible kids to do all the work; and you don't want to spend valuable time deciding who will do what. Begin by listing all the chores that need to be done. This includes everything from cooking to cleaning up when it is time to leave. Then you may assign all jobs. This way you can group people together for shared jobs. (You run the risk of complaints of favoritism here.) Or you can write all the jobs on pieces of paper and let everyone draw them out of a hat. Another method is to list the jobs on a poster and let them sign up for one or two themselves.

Keep the schedule simple. Allow ample time for food preparation and clean up. And remember the unique needs of your group for structure and for free time.

Keep in mind how much food teenagers need, especially in terms of snacks. Balance the amount of traditional adolescent junk food with healthy food for meals and snacks. Remember how much physical activity young people need. Keep physically active events as part of even the most serious activities.

Use young people's music to your advantage. Designate times when they can play their music, but limit the number of radios and tape players which can be playing at once. On certain kinds of retreats, you are justified in prohibiting all radios or tape players. Weave popular music into worship and discussion. Use it as a kickoff for special ideas. Make sure you consult with youth leadership about just what is popular at the time if you are going to use contemporary music to make a point.

Always keep the environment safe, physically and emotionally. Friendly horseplay easily gets out of hand, so be ready to limit it. Make sure waterfront activities are supervised. Do not let the group be cruel to any of its members, whether that be by constant physical harassment or the kind of emotional harassment of using derogatory nicknames or jokes.

Use short times of silence and meditation. Candles, a bonfire, water become powerful spiritual symbols which convey their grace with few words. Communion shared on a retreat in times set aside for silence and reflection has special meaning. Trust the symbols.

Remember re-entry. First, be aware that the reunion of young people with parents often carries some conflict with it. One may be tired or grouchy. The other may be enthusiastic and elated. Help both parents and young people be ready for ways to regather. For example, help parents to greet their young people positively rather than with phrases like, "The first thing you need to do is clean your room and then catch up on the homework you missed." And when parents do inquire as to what happened on the retreat, help the young people to be ready with some stories and descriptions that convey the experience rather than monosyllabic grunts.

The "real world" is tough after the rarefied atmosphere of the retreat. Plan transitional activities at the end of the retreat. Enable the young people to start thinking of how they will take their learnings home with them before they leave. You may give them a symbol of the retreat to take home. A small cross, a T-shirt with a design reflecting the theme of the retreat, or a hand-lettered personal scripture passage are all take-home items that bridge the gap.

Finally, arrive home when you said you would get there. Affirm to the parent the positive role their young person played on the retreat. Thank all the helpers, and plan some compensatory rest time for yourself. If you are a staff member at the church, take the next day off. You deserve it. If you are employed outside the church, do your best to have an easy day for yourself. You need time both to rest and enjoy reflecting on this special event.

Chapter 12
Sample Youth-Group Retreats

W e have discussed the overview of planning retreats for high-school groups. Several sample youth-group retreats follow. Each is designed to fulfill a certain goal for a given youth group. You can use these themes to address your own goals, or let these sample programs generate ideas which suit the unique nature of your own group.

The Web

The goals for this retreat are to provide an opportunity for the young people to experience some personal growth and some affirmation of their own gifts; to reflect on their friendships and relationships; and to allow the members of the group to get better acquainted, forming a sense of themselves as a group. This overnight is very simple. It can be used with any size group at any time the group needs to go back to those first levels of group building.

The retreat begins with arrival at the retreat center in mid-morning. Immediately after arrival and the unloading of the cars, the young people are sent out in groups of twos and threes to explore the camp. They are given fifteen minutes to do their exploration. When they return, there is a snack waiting for them (bagels, apples, and cider). Then have them gather together as a group (if you have a large youth group, you can split into several smaller groups at any of the group gatherings). Have a large piece of newsprint and markers. Appoint a recorder. The group will then attempt to make a map of the campground by what they have seen on their explorations, instructing the recorder as to where various things are. This is a good exercise in learning group co-operation and listening skills; it can be a lot of fun. It also orients everyone to where they are and to what recreational facilities are available. About fifteen to twenty minutes is sufficient for this exercise.

The next part of the retreat focuses on relationships with friends. Allow about one and a half to two hours. It consists of several activities, explained below, which help to focus on friendships and also on the youth group itself. All the activities can be used, or some can be omitted, but they are listed in an intentional order.

a) Ask everyone in the group to stand up and move to an area of the room where there is no furniture. Then tell them that the center of that space represents the center, or the hub, of the youth group. They are to sit on the floor in a place which represents where they feel they are in the youth group (in the center, on the fringe, partly in, whatever). Take a piece of masking tape and put in in front of each young person; ask them to write their name on the tape. Do not discuss this activity at all at this point. Simply ask everyone to look around and see where everyone is.

b) Group Connections. This next exercise works well for a group of eight to twenty. A larger group would need to be subdivided, as it would take too long. Use a large ball or brightly colored yarn. While the young people are still sitting from the first exercise, toss the yarn to someone in the group. They are then to toss it to each person they have spoken with on a one-to-one basis that morning. In a large group you could have more than one ball of yarn being tossed at a time. Once one person is finished, the yarn goes to the next person. The net result looks like a spider's web of yarn, and it reveals something about the connections among the people in the group.

c) Friendship Scavenger Hunt. Give each young person a pencil and the following list. They have ten or fifteen minutes (depending on the size of the group) to see how many signatures they can get. When they find a person who fits the category, that person is to sign their sheet. You can have music playing in the background for this. It is good to have them up and moving around.

Friendship Scavenger Hunt

1. Find someone who has more friends now than when s/he was in elementary school.
2. Find someone who has a good friend (not a girlfriend or a boyfriend in the romantic sense) of the opposite sex.
3. Find someone who has a pen pal or who has written to someone from another country.
4. Find someone who has a friend whom they've been friends with since they were five years old.
5. Find someone who has made a new friend this year (since school started).
6. Find someone who has a friend (not a relative) who is ten years old or younger.
7. Find someone who has all the friends they want to have.
8. Find someone who thinks it was easier to make friends when s/he was younger.
9. Find someone who has a friend (not a relative) who is over sixty years old.
10. Find someone who worked through an argument or a real disagreement with a friend—and they are still friends now.
11. Ask someone this question: "If you could be friends with anyone in the world, who would you choose?" Record their answer.

At the end of the allotted time, you can give a mint or piece of gum to everyone who has each item signed. Then have everyone stand up who fits each category. Ask each young person in turn "What was one thing you learned about yourself and your own friendships in the process of this scavenger hunt?"

d) The Super Friend. Take a giant sheet of newsprint; appoint a recorder who is furnished with a package of good colored markers. The group then verbally instructs the recorder on how to draw a picture of someone who is a Super Friend. The young people are to think of qualities and characteristics that would make someone a perfect friend and then find a way to represent those traits on the picture. This is a really fun way to have a discussion of what makes a good friend. Another way to do this is to have each young person make his or her own collage about what a good friend is and does.

e) Friendship Survey. Give each person a copy of the chart below and a pencil. They are to sit somewhere privately for about

Friendship Survey

Name	How is this person like you? Different from you?	How did you meet? Who initiated the friendship?

What do you receive from this person?	What do you give to this person?	Is this friendship nourishing or draining?

Finish these two sentences after you have filled in the chart and thought about your answers:

1) Two things I have learned about my friendships are _____

_____.

2) I'm glad that I _____.

fifteen minutes. They should pick three or four of their friends and list their names or initials on the left column. They will fill out the chart about each of those friends, and what they write will be private. They will not be asked to share it. Then they should write answers to the two questions on the botton of the page.

When the time is up, have the young people regather in groups of six to eight. Let them each share their answers to the questions on the bottom of the page. Most likely some discussion of friendships will evolve from the sharing. You can facilitate this discussion, but do not keep it going artificially.

Next on the schedule is lunch and a good break of free time. When a retreat begins in the morning, and meals are not furnished by the retreat center, an easy alternative for lunch is to have the young people bring their own lunch. You can then furnish drinks and dessert. Other easy lunch options include: peanut butter and jelly sandwiches or make-your-own submarine sandwiches from a supply of lunch meat and rolls.

The morning session has been long and very focused. It is good to give a substantial break at this point. The young peole need time together for recreation and relaxation which is less structured. It is better to give a long block of time so that they can do things like hike or canoe or swim than to have a lot of small adult-style coffee breaks. A two-hour break after lunch is not unreasonable if there are good recreational facilities where you are. And, of course, when they come back from the break, you'll need to have a snack waiting for them. Gatorade is a great thirst-quencher; fruit and munchies like pretzels go over well also.

Allow approximately two to two-and-a-half hours for the afternoon session on "Relationships with Friends and Families." In this session, some exercises from Transactional Analysis work well to show how we can block ourselves from having honest workable relationships. First, explain the difference between clear straight transactions and crooked twisted transactions. A game, in Transactional Analysis, is a crooked transaction between people that is repeated over and over again. There are three roles that people can play in these games: victim, persecutor, and rescuer.

Divide the group into subgroups. Give each small group one of the following role plays to dramatize and some time to work on it. When each group presents their role play, the other young people watch it to try to identify who is the victim, who is the persecutor, and who is the rescuer. You can then have some discussion on the situation itself. where have they seen it before? Who do they identify with?

a) Game: "Why Don't You—Yes, But."

-Victim: You have an English paper due on Monday which you haven't started. You want to go to the beach with your friends, but your parents won't let you go with the paper undone. It is after school on Friday, and you meet with your English teacher to get an extension. Your friend, who is going to the beach with you, comes along for moral support. Your teacher is unbending; your friend keeps making suggestions which you reject with excuses.

-Rescuer: You are the friend who keeps trying to help. You say "Well, why don't you . . .", trying to find solutions for your friend and even compromises for the teacher. Your friend responds to every suggestion of yours with an excuse, saying "Yes, but . . . ."

-Presecutor: You are the teacher who stands firm with your assignment. You offer no help at all.

b) Game: "Wooden Leg."

-Victim: You are at a party with some friends. They invite you to play volleyball, but you don't want to play so you say you have a sore thumb. Then they start dancing. You don't think you dance well, so you say you have a bad knee. When they decide to go swimming, you say you have a cold. You have an excuse for yourself for everything you don't want to do.

-Rescuer: You are the friend who keeps trying to help. You offer ice for the sore thumb, a chair for the bad knee, kleenex for the cold. You are not trying to find a solution; you just keep pampering your friend.

-Persecutor: You are the friend who constantly bugs the victim about every excuse, giving him/her a hard time about sitting around and doing nothing.

c) Game: "See What You Made Me Do." (The roles change in this game; the trick is to see who shifts roles and when.)

1st person—You are a teenager, playing your records on the good stereo in the living room. Your mother tells you three times to stop playing the records and to go to your room and do your homework. The first two times you promise to quit in just a minute. The third time she screams at you; you hit the needle on the stereo and scratch the record. You scream back at her "See what you made me do."

2nd person—You are the mother trying to get your teenager to start on homework. You play the scene as above, after which you return to the kitchen to cut up vegetables for the salad.

3rd person—You are the younger brother or sister, having overheard the scene above. You walk into the kitchen saying "What was that all about?" Mom cuts her finger with the knife and yells at you, "See what you made me do!"

d) Game: "Uproar."

Five people are at a family dinner: mother, father, one teenage daughter, one younger sibling, and a grandparent. Mother tries to begin a conversation about planning for summer vacation. Younger sibling joins in happily. The teenager thinks it all sounds boring and doesn't want to go. The father then jumps all over the daughter for being spoiled and ungrateful. Daughter fights back. Mother defends father; younger child keeps getting more and more sweet and wonderful. The grandparent tries to rescue the daughter, who then stomps out of the room yelling "No one understands me around here," and slams the door. Father follows daughter shouting, "Nobody slams doors in this house and goes unpunished." Mother says, "Now this meal is ruined." Younger child tells mother, "I liked the meal anyway." Grandmother says to mother, "We certainly didn't let our children act this way when you were young."

After the group has watched the games, see if they can suggest how someone could have intervened in each situation to make the transaction more honest and clear and less of a game. A good resource for Transactional Analysis is the book *Born To Win* by James and Jongeward (Addison Wesley, 1971).

Another series of role plays which are fun to do with teenagers and which focus on family relationships are called "Bringing On Your Parent." First, explain how everyone has within them parts of their personality which are their child, parts which are their parent, and parts which are their adult. There are situations which call forth each of these three parts. Announce that we are going to role play some ways in which teenagers can guarantee that they will bring out the parent, rather than the adult, in anyone. Divide them into groups of two or three; one is the teenager, one is the parent, and the third can be the other parent or a sibling. Tell them to act out the following situations with the teenager taking the leading part and the others reacting:

a) Complaining. You are hungry, you are cold, your foot hurts; just complain and keep complaining. Watch what happens with those around you.

b) Showing indecision. At a restaurant trying to decide what to eat; or at a store trying to decide on new clothes; or trying to decide whether to go on a youth-group overnight.

c) Breaking the rules. Come home two hours late without having called.

d) Refusing to answer. Whatever the parent says, refuse to answer. Just look away or walk away.

e) Playing stupid. You are asked to sweep the floor. You play stupid—where's the broom; how do you sweep?; where should I put it?

f) Being careless. Break something of value because you were not being careful.

g) Facial expressions or gestures. Curled lip, wrinkled nose, glaring, etc. in response to an adult.

These are very funny role plays with the young people acting out all the roles. They will enjoy doing it and watching it. They can identify immediately with what gets the parent going, and they will be able to talk about where they see themselves. A discussion can follow about how to avoid getting into these emotional overloads with parents. Another twist is to talk about what parents can say or do that guarantees the young person will act like a child.

It is important to end this session with each young person sharing something they learned about themselves or about their families. You need to clarify the difference between these games and real straight conversations and transactions, especially pointing out the rewards for adult interactions.

After this session, a round of volleyball or other group game feels good. And then it will be time for dinner. If the campground provides meals, that is great. If you are in a location where you can send out for chicken or pizza, that works well. If you have to cook yourselves, keep it simple and fun. Barbecuing hamburgers on a grill; warming lasagna that was made at home; making individual pizzas on split hoagie rolls are all easy and well-accepted by teens. Teens love salads when they can fix their own like a salad bar. You can fill them up with lots of good bread. You may want to take a half-hour break after dinner.

Group games are fun in the early evening. There are good game resources listed in the appendix. One fun game for a retreat on this theme has everyone writing down on a piece of paper something the group does not know about them. You collect these, read them aloud, and everyone tries to guess who it is. Group singing works well in the evening. Just be sure to have enough songbooks or songsheets so that everyone has a copy of the words to the songs.

The evening is a good time for spiritual reflection and specific religious input. There isn't the restlessness to get outside for sports or swimming. The atmosphere can be quieted with candles, a fire in the fireplace, or soft lighting. On this retreat, Bible study followed singing and prepared for communion.

A good method for Bible study with young people is that developed by Walter Wink in *Transforming Bible Study* (Abingdon, 1980). Wink uses an open-ended questioning approach based on the thesis that the biblical word of God always seeks to transform the life of the reader. Wink suggests exploring passages with as many questions as possible about the nature of God suggested here, the consciousness of the actors in the stories, and the experiences of the first hearers of these stories. In posing these questions, solicit as many answers as possible without indicating that any particular answer is right or wrong. The purpose is to open the heart to the spirit moving here.

An exploration of John 15:11-17, where Jesus says "The greatest love a person can have for his friends is to give his life for them. And you are my friends if you do what I command you." (John 15:14-15, TEV), suggests the following questions for discussion.

1. What do you think of when you picture God as the master and you as the servant?

2. How does that remind you of some of the parent-child transactions we role-played earlier?

3. What is the difference between the relationship of a master to a servant and a friend to a friend?

4. Have you ever had a teacher, a parent, an adult, or someone you looked up to call you a friend?

5. Did you believe them? Why? Why not?

6. How does a friend behave to really be a friend?

7. Jesus says that he calls you friend, that he chose you. How does Jesus happen to choose you as a friend?

8. If Jesus is your friend, then is your friend Jesus?

9. Are you Jesus to a friend? How?

10. Jesus says, "I call you friends . . . . I chose you and appointed you to go and bear much fruit, the kind of fruit that endures." (vs. 15, 16.) What kind of friend is Jesus calling you to be? How will you answer? (Go around the circle and give everyone an opportunity to answer.)

Move from Bible study into worship and communion. Begin worship by asking everyone to close their eyes and imagine a time that day when they felt completely alone. Feel that isolation and aloneness. Stay in that isolation for a few minutes in silence. Then ask them to take the hand of the person on either side. Feel the connection of friendship, a link with the friendship of God. Sing "Kum Ba Yah" with their hands linked.

Share the bread of communion. As each person receives the bread around the circle, ask each young person to share "a time this weekend when someone reached out to me in friendship . . . ." Next, share the cup of wine with a guided meditation about God's call to each person and their responses. Close the time of worship according to your tradition.

After worship, you can have a snack, a night hike, a good game of charades, a movie, whatever suits your group for a late-night activity.

Our retreat ended by midmorning the next day, so we had one more group session. In this session, designate a part of the room to represent the youth group, pointing out where the center is, and ask the young people to sit in a place again which represents where they feel they are in the group this morning. Then let each of them share about where they sat yesterday, where they are sitting today, and what the difference is.

Give each young person a ball of yarn. They are to throw it from themselves to every other person they had a one-to-one interaction with during the retreat. Compare the web today with the interactions yesterday. Talk about their connections as a group.

Then give each young person a symbol of the weekend to take home: a T-shirt; a poster; a Bible passage; whatever. Do this slowly and individually. As it is each person's turn to receive his or her symbol, ask everyone else in the group to tell that person one thing about him/her that makes him/her a good friend. This is a form of verbal gift-giving which affirms the positive qualities of each young person in turn. You may want to end this session with a song and with hugs. (Since meals and games are covered thoroughly in the description of this retreat, we will not repeat this information again under each sample retreat. Between every session, however, there is something to eat and either free time or active group games.)

"SUPERPOWERS"

This is a more complex youth group overnight. It revolves around a simulation expereince, an illusion which everyone in the group pretends is real. Our simulation was based on the movie "Superman I." In that movie, the planet Krypton was about to be destroyed. Jor-El and his wife decided to send their son to another planet where he might survive. With him, they sent messages and ways for him to recover the powers of his heritage. In our simulation, the illusion is that our planet is on the verge of destruction. Members of the youth group have been chosen to be among a small group of young people who will be given passage to another solar system where they may preserve and realize their superpowers. They are cautioned that everyone must participate in the illusion and pretend that it is real for the weekend to work.

The retreat begins with an escape. The young people are told that they must meet at a secret rendezvous for their transport. This escape can be as elaborate as you choose. They can have a sealed envelope sent to their parents to open the morning of the overnight, which contains instructions and directions for finding the escape site. These directions can be simple; they can be coded; they can be like a treasure hunt. The more imagination you can provide here, the more fun they will have. Sample directions follow:

"Go to the Krystal hamburger place on University Avenue. Wear a blue shirt and sunglasses. Order something to drink with two straws. By 9:20, be sitting in a booth by the window, with the two straws in your drink. Your contact will approach you and will say, 'I'll share if you will share.' The message below will help both of you figure out where to go next: "G T T E F L Z (H C U E T B C L E H R E'). G T T E A O S O T E E.

"Bring: a sleeping bag, a lunch, a flashlight, a bathing suit, a Bible, casual clothes and toilet articles. Also bring one thing that is very important to you personally, something that you would take if you really were going to a new planet. Remember that you will have to carry everything that you bring and you will be walking with it for quite a distance.

"If you get lost or miss your contacts, call this number for further instructions: _____."

The contact person will have a message which reads: O O H U P A A (W I H S D O E A L D A D E S). O O H G T R H P H R. When you put the two messages together properly, they read "Go to the UF Plaza (which used to be called Hardee's). Go to the Gator Shop there."

After you arrive at your destination and get settled, the first session begins with an explanation of the theme. "Superman discovers during his growing years that he has powers which are unique. Each of us has superpowers of our own that are unequaled anywhere else. The purpose of life is to discover those powers and to learn how to use them for all that is good, and beautiful, and true, to learn how to use them for the good of the world and of humanity. Our purpose this weekend, on this new planet, is to discover our powers, to learn how to use them, and to affirm others. To do this, we will listen to each other, do nothing to hurt or put down anyone else, and spend time seriously thinking about ourselves and our lives." If your group is not familiar with the story of Superman, you may want to begin the weekend by showing the movie. If the story is familiar, you can start the first session with a meditative prayer, learning how to center yourselves and how to locate your center of being.

Next, distribute a small tape recorder and a tape to each young person, which they will take to a place by themselves so that they can listen to the tape privately. Each young person has a tape which was made ahead of time by his/her parent(s). On this ten-minute tape, the parents were asked to include a sense of their child's background and family heritage; their hopes for their child as s/he was born or adopted; the significance of their child's name; and what they wish for their child's life in the future as an adult. This parallels the experience of Superman in his journey to earth. When the group comes back together after listening, ask each person to share one thing they learned from the tape. Then ask each person to share the special thing they brought with them from home that they would want to have in a new world.

In the afternoon session, the participants focus on the power of their personalities by looking at their Clark Kent self and their Superman self. This links very nicely with the scripture passage 2 Corinthians 4:7, where we are told that we have a spiritual treasure in common clay pots. Ask the young people to write down several occasions in the past year when they can remember feeling like or doing something like Clark Kent. Ask them to do the same thing in terms of Superman. Then ask them to share one incident from each list. Another good question to pose is "What is your Kryptonite? What is something which keeps you from using your superpowers?"

This retreat is also a good opportunity to talk about sex and sexual powers. You can decide whether or not to include this topic in the weekend. Use of an attitude or values questionnaire can be helpful. You ask the young people to fill out the questionnaire before the session, indicating only whether they were a boy or girl. You collate the results by the boys' answers, by the girls' answers, and for the group as a whole. When you get to the session, you simply present the collation of answers as a way to get discussion going on the topics. The young people seem to talk more readily when they see how the group feels or how the boys or girls answered. You can focus the conclusion of the discussion on how each of us has choices about how to use our sexual powers and how important those choices are.

Another power to emphasize is our power to laugh and have fun. You may use a game like Charades to call up this power. You may simply want to have fun and experience that; you may want to have a short session where you talk and share about this power.

Evening worship focuses on spiritual powers. Talk about spiritual power being real and realizable, around you and within you. It is a force that can energize you, heal you, calm you, and protect you, if you are open to it. Throughout the ages, people of all races and religions have been aware of the tremendous potentials of spiritual power. Try a guided meditation or prayer which focuses on their spiritual power. At this point, you might consider having a resource person appear, someone who has something special to share about spiritual power. We used a young man who was well trained in karate. He was able to speak about his internal powers and how he saw them in a spiritual context. He demonstrated by breaking a thick board with his hands. It was very impressive. Communion can follow as a time to share spiritual needs and promises. Close communion with songs and hugs.

In the final session, have a blank piece of paper for every person with their names on it. Put these papers on a table or hang them up around the room. Give everyone a pencil or marker. Each person is to write on every other person's paper a strength they see that person having. When it is over, each person will have a list of their powers in writing, as they are observed by everyone else in the group. Close with a blessing of each young person, individually by name. Sometimes, if the group is in the right mood, you can do lifting here. Have the person stand up and slowly lean back. Everyone else in the group puts a hand underneath the person from toe to head and slowly lifts him/her up over their heads. If you gently rock them back and forth, it feels (almost) like flying. It is a wonderful sensation—a powerful ending.

This theme of personal powers can be attached to other movies or stories as well. You could use it as "Yoda's Cave" and hook onto the popular Star Wars sagas. "The Empire Strikes Back" is available in paperback and has a number of excellent quotations about discovering "The Force" within. To some extent, "Rocky" might fit. The biblical David is a natural tale of the possibilities and pitfalls of special gifts of strength. You'll probably think of others.

"FEAR AND RISK"

This is also a simulation where we ask the young people to act as if the experience we are constructing were really happening. Our purpose in this simulation is to explore how well we do in standing for our faith in the face of political repression and to use this process as a group building experience. Here is the simulation we present to the young people:

> This is a time in our country of a totalitarian government. The purpose of this government is to create a population of uniform beliefs. Little by little, a form of mind and thought control has been imposed on the populace. Newspapers, radio, and TV are controlled by the state. There is a state religion, which has been decreed as the appropriate means to progress. Anything which stands in the way of progress is outlawed by the government.
>
> Communities of resistance throughout the land have refused to give in to the god of uniformity. Your church is one of those resistance communities, and, as a member of your church, the state has declared you an outlaw. Word

has been received of a massive arrest planned for the weekend and leaders of the youth group have planned an escape to a safe hideout.

With this information, the youth group members are again given instructions for their escape. As in the "Super Powers" retreat, these instructions can be as simple or elaborate as you wish to make them. We also warn them that members of the state "police" may try to apprehend members of the group. The rule is that if an "identified police person" makes any physical contact with them, they are to consider themselves captured and make no attempt to escape.

All of this is explained clearly to the parents in a separate letter. The parents are told where the retreat will be held, but are asked not to tell the young people of the location.

As the young people participate in their escape, a few are "captured and detained." Here it is very important to be careful about who acts as police and who is detained. Use caring and compassionate adult church members to act as "police." Their job is to pretend and *only* pretend to be enforcers of the "totalitarian state rules." Remember how easy it is for actors in guard and prison simulations to forget they are role playing and start living their parts. Also capture only those members of your group who are secure enough to handle being caught. At any sign of undue stress, end the simulation.

In a group of about twenty-five young people, you may want to "capture" four or five. These detainees are taken back to the church and questioned while the other group members go to the retreat site. The detainees are given a "Form for Attitude Improvement" from "The Federal Board of Religious Development," which they are to fill out. The form asks their name, age, address, religious institution of which they are a member, why they joined, and if they accept the beliefs of this group. They are then asked to sign a release renouncing their former religious beliefs and accepting the religious premises of the state such as:

God is known in only one way: by the fruits of progress. Religion is an individual matter between the person and the state; the gathering together for religious purposes is prohibited unless the gathering is sanctioned by the state. The past is irrelevant for our technological age; the future cannot be known; the present is all that matters. To follow Jesus is to work for progress and the common good as defined by state programs; people who are weak are a burden to the state and to God.

You may develop your own statement which directly contradicts familiar teachings of your church. All the young person has to do is sign the release, renouncing their former beliefs, and they are told that they can join their friends on their retreat.

While a few young people have been detained, the rest of the group has been transported, preferably in a closed van, to a "hideout." Upon arrival they get unpacked, explore the surroundings, check for food (which has been conveniently hidden in the building previously). They discover that some of their members are missing.

All of this takes quite a while. Soon the "captured" members are brought to the group by their captors. These guards may then question other group members about their faith, again with the promise that they will be allowed to continue their weekend away if they just renounce their faith.

In developing this simulation, we cannot overemphasize keeping limits upon it. Do not be overly manipulative or the level of frustration and anger will get out of control. It is also important that the political repression described not be something as clichéd as "godless communism" or "Arab terrorists." The scenario should be a totalitarianism that combines the extremes of both left- and right-wing ideology. This beginning has quite an impact, but it should not be carried out too long.

Debriefing should begin soon. Quite a bit of tension can be released in sharing stories of the escape and letting those who were caught tell the stories of their interrogation. Young people are quite tenacious in sticking with their beliefs in the face of this pressure. They should be affirmed for following their faith through this simulation experience. Take time for each young person to explain how he or she felt during the different stages of the escape. Ask for good times and bad times in the experience. Then let everyone have a chance to share something they learned about themselves and their faith in this experience. Follow this with extended time for recreation.

When you return to discussions on the subject matter, follow the theme of fear and risk.

Two bible study possibilities go along with this theme. I John 4:18, states, "There is no fear in love; perfect love drives out all fear." The opposite of love may not be hate, but fear, according to this passage. Explore the implications of this statement. Look at the ways in which love is an antidote to fear. How did the love, which is the community of their youth group, get them through the fear of the escape and interrogation? How does love combat political repression? How does love confront power?

A second Bible study experience is the story of the raising of Lazarus, from John 11. This exercise has been used in Lyman Coleman's *Serendipity* series (Creative Resources, 1968-1974) as well as other Bible study guides. Read the story of Lazarus and emphasize that when Lazarus was called forth from the dead, Jesus asked those around to untie his grave cloths. Then designate one young person to be Lazarus. This person sits in front of the group on a chair. Distribute strips of cloth, such as torn-up sheets, to each person present and give them a magic marker. Ask them to write something on their cloth which represents a fear. Give them several specific examples, such as a fear of being alone or a fear of risking more of themselves with this youth group. They then wrap their cloths around Lazarus until he or she is covered. Let them picture Lazarus bound in death by their fears. The leader reads the end of the story again, ending with "(Jesus) called out in a loud voice, 'Lazarus, come out!' He came out, his hands and feet wrapped in grave cloths, and with a cloth around his face. 'Untie him,' Jesus told them, 'and let him go.' " (John 11:43-44, TEV). Group members then approach Lazarus one by one and untie the cloths, each reading the cloth he or she unties. This will not necessarily be the cloth they put on Lazarus.

To close the session, ask each person what they learned in doing the exercise. Usually common themes and fears develop and participants find that they are not alone in their fears. Make sure to take time to let Lazarus explain how he or she felt being wrapped and unwrapped.

After an experience such as this, there should be a break for games or snacks. Close the evening with communion, perhaps inviting participants to pray for ways they can risk more of themselves in love and faith.

End the retreat with a focus on the blessings of second chances, resurrections, and the current freedom we have to live our faith. This is a good time for the young people to make a covenant about how they will continue living the convictions they discovered within themselves during the weekend.

"THE CRYSTAL RIVER DISASTER"

This is another simulation. The goal is to provide an intensive group building experience focusing heavily on the here and now. It is not an experience for a loosely connected youth group. Its secondary goal is to develop a concern for the environment and the threats to it.

To do this we created a simulation of a nuclear power plant meltdown. The nearest one to us happens to be the Crystal River Nuclear Reactor about fifty miles away. (This retreat was developed before Three Mile Island or Chernobyl, so the threat seemed rather innocuous at the time.) Concern for the safety of nuclear power plants is truly a secondary issue of this overnight, but, if the nuclear threat might overtake the group process, perhaps a less frightening scenario could be developed. It may be more relevant to use a danger close to home, a nearby chemical plant, a climactic inversion from local pollutants, or even a natural disaster such as a hurricane or flood.

The young people receive instructions for the overnight. These instructions have been mailed to their parents, but the young people are not allowed to open them until one hour before they leave. There is a description of what a simulation is and how they are to enter the illusion. Then they read the following message:

> There have been rumors for the past week that the Crystal River Nuclear Power plant was having technical difficulties and that radioactive steam has been leaking slowly into the air. This morning, Larry Reimer received a call from a friend who works at the Gainesville *Sun* who had gone to the Crystal River plant last week to meet an employee willing to talk with him. The reporter discovered that the situation was much worse than the press had been told and that the amount of radioactivity leaking into the air has been increasing each day. Larry was told by the reporter that if the leak could not be controlled by this morning, it would start a chain reaction which might mean nuclear disaster. Shortly after he received this information, Larry was told by a Civil Defense official that as part of Stage Alpha he was to alert members of his church youth group. In the event of an impending disaster, a three-tiered plan goes into effect. Stage Alpha is to evacuate young people and pregnant women to holding areas outside the city as

a preliminary precaution. Stage Beta is when the general public is informed and told to prepare for possible evacuation. Stage Gamma is when the general public is evacuated to sealed shelters. We are now in Stage Alpha alert. You are to report to the following location for transport to a safe area.

Young people are then informed to bring what they need to survive for twenty-four hours, but not more than they can carry by themselves. They should include something they would be willing to put in a time capsule (which will not be returned).

The entry to this event is not hurried. The first vans take them to a pleasant house just outside of town. They put their gear away, share experiences of leaving and something of what they brought. There is time for games and the atmosphere is rather relaxed.

Then a uniformed person arrives with bad news that further evacuation is necessary. Participants are taken to another site in a van with a taped civil defense message playing on the tape deck.

They are taken to a blocked off section of the church. All windows are covered. Bathrooms are accessible. They are given decontaminated scrub suits to wear and checked by a doctor. They enter a large room where they are to sit quietly until all are present. A simulated radio broadcast is played where the extent of the emergency is described and everyone is told to stay in their evacuation quarters for either twelve or twenty-four hours, depending on your own schedule. Just as it begins to get dark, all electric power goes out.

Now is the time to focus on exactly what the group will do with themselves. Have them share what they brought and what they were thinking of when they brought it. How many people brought food? Did anyone bring water, flashlights, or candles? Some young people will have thought of this. Most will not. It is a good idea to stock your "shelter" with staples, enough candles to make it through your allotted time, bread, peanut butter and jelly, even bottled water.

The goal of most growth groups is to get people to focus on the here and now and explore their decision-making patterns. You now have the perfect environment for this process. The next 12-24 hours are up to the young people. The group will have to decide when and what to eat, how to apportion the food for the rest of the period. When will they sleep? How will they make decisions?

You will have to help them process how they are making decisions. Some groups have spent hours deciding how to eat dinner, whether they would all pool their food, or whether those who brought their own would eat their own while the others divided up the peanut butter. It is important to help them learn through this process and then make sure they have time for breaks and games.

After a good break, return for some serious discussions. Have the young people write stories of who they are and what they have done with their lives. Share what they brought for the time capsule, and actually make a time capsule which can be kept in the church for 10-20 years. Write a group story of what went wrong in the world that brought us to this place and seal it in the time capsule. Have participants write a letter to themselves, "If I had more time, I would . . . ."

Share communion as a possibility for new life and let each person share one line from their letter as they receive the bread. As the cup is passed, let all the members of the group share a strength they have seen in the person receiving the cup, one at a time. Collect the letters to mail as a post-retreat follow up. Take time for silence and reflection.

Prepare a latenight taped news broadcast. If you are having a twelve-hour alert, have a morning broadcast announcing that the disaster has been averted. Celebrate this new possibility for life and continue events accordingly.

You may follow this kind of program in a variety of settings to varying degrees. It can be done, as described here, at a room in the church, sealing off the outside world as much as possible. Or you can go to a retreat center in an isolated area. If the retreat is more than one night, do not try to maintain the simulation with total intensity all the time. Even on a short retreat, there should be breaks for games and relaxation.

The content of the disaster is not as important as the sense of building community from scratch. Thus, if nuclear or pollution disaster becomes too threatening emotionally, consider a shipwreck, Swiss Family Robinson setting, anything that throws the group back on its own resources.

This is an exciting retreat, but it is not always easy to maintain. A lot of stress can build up, and leaders need to nurture the group as well. When it is over, participants uniformly report it as an excellent learning experience.

Give the participants something like a T-shirt which says, "I survived CRD." This becomes a way they can share their experiences with others who inquire. As with all simulations, learning and experiences need to be constantly processed and debriefed.

Summary Reflections

The primary theme of this survey of youth group retreats, from the very general to the specific, is to plan well and to keep the activities varied. There is always talk about how young people just want to be entertained. Youth organizations react with more work and structure. The typical young person in the church youth group has a long day at school, especially if any extracurricular activities such as clubs, music, or sports are added on. There is the constant pressure of grades. Young people need to have fun together in a safe environment. At the same time, they need the challenge of exploring their beliefs and values. The outlines of retreats offered here attempt to keep this balance.

This framework can be applied to any issue which the young people face, whether that is sexuality or discerning God's call. Many of these ideas can also be used with middle school or junior high youth group, but whenever you deal with this age group, simplify the discussion and increase the recreational events. It is always difficult to know whether overnights for junior highs are pushing them too soon so that there is nothing exciting to look forward to in high school. Evaluate the maturity of your young people. If they can't wait for their own overnight, offer one, but on a highly abbreviated basis.

Youth group retreats are probably some of the most crucial experiences in a person's developing faith in God and discovery of self. The experiences of a youth-group retreat cannot be duplicated in any other setting. Memories of these events last a lifetime.

Section III
The Small-Group Adult Retreat

Introduction

Small-group retreats are a joy. Their size is easily managed; they can be intimate and relaxed, and they are ready vehicles for spiritual growth and nurture. While the programs offered at these retreats may differ widely in structure and purpose, there are common ways of planning and organizing them.

The small-group retreat is one in which there is a minimum of ten and a maximum of twenty-five persons attending. With this size in mind, we will offer a general background for planning small-group retreats, followed by guidelines for four types of retreats. The first type of overnight is for people with a common bond, such as a men's, women's, couple's, or single's retreat. The second variety is the spiritual retreat in the classic Roman Catholic tradition as well as with some of the recent modifications for mainline Protestant participants. The third kind of retreat is one on a particular theme or subject. A special fourth section is provided by Jack M. Everitt of the Everitt and Associates Management and Leadership Firm on leadership development and program planning for church boards and committees.

Chapter 13

Initial Planning and Arrangements

I t is helpful to identify your purpose or goal at the initial stages of planning. Small-group retreats can be designed for any of the following goals: for spiritual growth or renewal; for learning about a particular topic; for fellowship and bonding between people; for a particular group of people who have something in common to discuss their shared issue; for relaxation and fun; and for planning and goal setting.

Once you have established your purpose for the retreat, then you are ready to proceed with a framework. You may want to draw one or two other people into the planning process. For a small-group retreat, we do not feel it is necessary to have a large or formal committee. It is something that one or two people (at the most three) can plan together. Whoever does the planning should be well acquainted with the people in the church and should feel comfortable working with the retreat's purpose.

One of the first decisions is how long the experience will be. Many retreats are designed to be a weekend experience, beginning on Friday evening and ending on Sunday. We have had very good experiences with overnights for small groups. Typically, these would begin with lunch on Saturday and end by noon on Sunday. It is often easier to get a group to commit themselves to one night than to a whole weekend. This framework also has another advantage. People have had a chance to go home from work on Friday, relax, do chores, and leave leisurely on Saturday morning. They then arrive at the retreat rested and ready to begin. They also then have time on Sunday to rejoin their family for afternoon and evening activities. However, if you want clergy leadership, the Friday evening to Saturday evening schedule allows the clergy person to be back for Sunday services.

The next question is where to have the retreat, and with small groups, there are many good options. Many camps and conference centers have facilities that are well suited for these retreats. Many denominational camps have separate lodges for small groups. However, find out in advance how much privacy you will have. You may not want to be next to a youth group.

Motels and condominiums are often a very good place for certain small-group retreats. You can often get a group discount on rooms as well as use of a meeting or conference room. Such a setting, if it is at a place like the mountains, a lake, or the ocean, can enhance the sense of relaxation and getting-away. Someone in the church might have a vacation place which would work well for a small group. Or you may be able to rent a lake or ocean house or a mountain cabin.

Wherever it is located, you will want a place that has as many of the following advantages as possible: a peaceful environment; places to walk alone; places to sit and think or talk; a comfortable, pleasant meeting room; good sleeping and bathroom facilities; somewhere to have relaxed communal meals; something which is naturally beautiful to look at (a lake, a pond, a valley, trees, flowers, whatever); minimal automobile traffic and congestion; no ringing telephones. The particular type of retreat will determine how much seclusion or privacy you need. The best choice is always to get away geographically from your usual home and church surroundings. However, for an overnight, you would not want to spend more than an hour and a half driving there. Don't be afraid to go to some place that is comfortable. Church leaders too often equate retreat with spartan. People enjoy getting away to a nice place.

The arrangement for meals will depend on the place you choose. Camps and conference centers will often provide meals for you, an extra we always take advantage of since it relieves everyone of time and responsibility before they come as well as during the retreat. Some retreat centers, condominiums, and lake houses will have a kitchen available. If you are going to prepare food, we recommend a pot-luck approach, where everyone brings something that is already fixed and only needs reheating or rearranging. If the group is between ten and sixteen people and there is a good restaurant available, eating dinner out together is also a viable fun option, although you should take cost and noise levels into account. On our small-group overnights, we often have people bring their own lunch, eat out together for dinner, and then serve a simple continental breakfast of fruit, breads, juice, and coffee or tea. These overnights are good times to provide a nurturing atmosphere of healthful snacks. Good breads, fruit, vegetables, and herbal teas set a wholistic tone. People not only feel better physically for having avoided junk food, but they are also proud of themselves for mentally breaking free of habit foods and drinks.

Leadership is the next issue. If the purpose of the retreat is spiritual renewal or growth, then you need a leader who is comfortable with spiritual direction. If the purpose is educational, you need a leader who has expertise in the topic. If the purpose is fellowship, sharing, getting to know each other, or personal growth, then you need a leader who is a good group facilitator. If the purpose is planning or leadership development, you need someone who is trained in these areas. The minister, a staff person, or a member of the congregation may be able to lead or you may have to find an outside resource person to take the leadership role. Whenever you use an outside leader, be sure that s/he understands the nature of the group and the kind of leadership you want.

The next step is to compute the expenses of the weekend. Add the charge for the rooms, plus whatever food you are providing, plus supplies, plus whatever you are paying the resource person. If the leader is not receiving a fee, his/her room and meals should be paid for by the group.

Target a specific group of people in the church who would benefit from such an experience and who would be good to have in the group. Send each of these people a personal letter, explaining the retreat as well as expressing your interest in having them attend. Here is a sample letter:

Dear Bob,

We are offering a small-group adult overnight which will focus on prayer. I thought this event might interest you.

The overnight will be held at Cedar Cove Condominiums at Cedar Key from midmorning on Saturday, January 22, to noon on Sunday, January 23. We intend for this to be a nurturing, nonstressful time for all who attend, with opportunities for sharing, silence, walks, fellowship, and being refreshed. There will be time to explore your thoughts and feelings about prayer, to talk together, and to experience various forms of prayers and meditations. The group will be limited to fifteen adults.

The cost will be $28 per person, plus the price of dinner at a restaurant.

Please let me know as soon as possible if you would be interested in attending this overnight. I will also be glad to hear any thoughts or suggestions you would have for the program. I look forward to hearing from you.

You can also make this invitation by phone. You are trying to develop a core group of six to sixteen people (depending on the size of your overnight) who will make a commitment to attend. Once you have a good core group, then you can open up the retreat to the wider church population and sign up anyone who is interested.

Chapter 14
Developing a Schedule

T he most important part of a good small-group retreat is fostering a relaxed nurturing atmosphere so that intimacy and trust can develop within the group. The first step in this process is the schedule. Whether you are meeting for one night or for a whole weekend, the pace needs to be calm, not frantic.

There are a number of ways to create a relaxed atmosphere, even in a one-night retreat. Ask people to arrive by 10:30 in the morning, which means that they have not had to get up terribly early and are rested. Have a nice snack with beverages awaiting their arrival so they begin by feeling expected, nurtured, and engaged in conversation. Allow plenty of time for arrival, so that no one feels late. Schedule some free time before and after each meal, especially dinner, so that people are not rushing from one activity to another.

In some settings and traditions, it would be appropriate to have wine and cheese available an hour before dinner. We have heard this referred to as the "mellow hour" or the "gracious hour." Dinner itself can be a very festive, relaxed, humorous occasion with lots of laughter and fun. There is no serious focus to the conversation, no agenda to achieve. Finish the evening session by 9:30 or 10:00, so that there is late-night time for people to talk individually, walk or get to sleep. The morning session is then from 9:30 to 11:00, with departure following, so that again people are not hurried. The main principles involved in scheduling decisions are to allow extra time between events, to schedule in free time and encourage people to use it in nurturing ways, and to have some group relaxation together.

A sample schedule follows:

SATURDAY

10:30—Arrive and check in
11:00—Group session #1
12:30—Lunch
 2:00—Group session #2
 4:00—Free time
 6:00—Dinner
 8:00—Group session #3
10:00—End of activities

SUNDAY

 8:30—Breakfast
 9:00—Group session #4 with closing worship
11:00—Pack and check out

Chapter 15

Developing Intimacy and Trust

I t is crucial in a small-group retreat to develop intimacy and trust within the group. The size of the group, the withdrawal from the everyday world, and the purpose of the weekend lend themselves to this kind of atmosphere.

Once you have a group of people signed up for the overnight, send a letter to them outlining all of the details, including what to bring and what to expect of the weekend. The tone of this letter sets the atmosphere for trust; it should be warm, and welcoming, and reassuring. A sample letter follows:

> To: Ed, Priscilla, Kevin, Madeline, Karen, Mary, Gene, Sandy, Carol, Tony, Jeanne, Pat, and Art

> Welcome to our small-group overnight on Psychosynthesis! I hope that you are looking forward to our time together as much as Larry and I are. As you can see, our group is full; in fact, we even have a waiting list. I am writing to let you know about the arrangements for the weekend, so that you can make your plans.

> Please arrive at the motel by 10:30 on Saturday morning, July 8; our program will begin at 11:00. We will finish on Sunday morning, July 9, at 11:00, so that you can be home shortly after noon. Cedar Cove is located on the Gulf. As you drive into Cedar Key, turn left onto Second Street and follow that street until you see Cedar Cove on the right. Go to the office to check in. If your room is not available, or after you get settled in your

room, please join us in room A-6. The phone number at Cedar Cove is 904-543-5332.

ROOMS—Each room has a bath, kitchen with table and chairs, desk, tv, phone, fold-out couch and two day beds. The kitchen is fully equipped with refrigerator, stove, toaster, dishes, pans and coffeemaker; there is no oven. The room charge will be $23 per person for 2 people in a room; $15.35 per person for 3 people in a room; or $11.50 per person for 4 people in a room.

MEALS—Please bring your own lunch, including a drink, for Saturday. We will go to the Seabreeze Restaurant as a group for dinner (the cost for dinners runs from $3.50 to $10.00 a person there). We will provide a continental breakfast of fruit, juice, hot beverages, and breakfast breads.

There will be an additional charge of $7 per person for the program portion and supplies. I need a deposit of $10.00 per person, plus an indication of your rooming preferences, by June 20. You may pay the rest when you arrive at Cedar Cove.

While we will spend a great deal of our time as a group exploring the concepts of Psychosynthesis, there will also be time to relax, to walk, to be alone. There is a swimming pool at the motel; there are tennis courts nearby.

Cedar Cove is a beautiful motel with a lovely view of the Gulf. It is a very restful place; just being there is a real treat. We look forward to enjoying it with you!

Each person should be greeted upon arrival, helped with arrangements and settling in, and given a sense of the schedule right away. This eliminates feelings of awkwardness and uncertainty, fostering instead a sense of structure and organization.

Begin the first session of every small-group overnight with a sincere welcome and appreciation of those who have come. Then go over the schedule for the retreat, asking for input or questions. The group itself may decide on a modification of the schedule, which is good. Sometimes it is helpful to leave parts of the schedule open, like the time for breakfast, and let the group set that time.

After those issues are covered, devote five or ten minutes to guidelines for group functioning. No matter how experienced your group is, these basics need to be articulated clearly at the beginning of the weekend. You may think of others to add. These are four basics:

1. Absolute confidentiality. Anything that is shared by anyone this weekend in the group remains with the group and is not to be shared at a later time with anyone else.
2. Sharing the group time fairly. Be conscious of giving everyone an equal turn to talk.
3. Responding with concern, not advice. Clarify what the person is saying, ask questions, and be empathetic. Try not to give advice unless the person specifically asks for it or agrees to it.
4. Sharing concerns or issues rather than telling long stories.
5. Permission to pass. When members of the group are asked to share personal experiences or concerns in turn, it should be understood that any individual has the right to say "I pass" without being challenged or questioned.

Discuss each one of these basics for good group dynamics to be sure that everyone understands them. This also signals that everyone in the group will help with the discussions rather than making the leaders solely responsible for how things go.

During the course of the retreat, the leader needs to monitor and implement these group understandings. There are several ways to be sure that everyone has an opportunity to talk. The simplest is to have times where there is a question or a concern which you ask each person to address in turn, going around the circle. This assures that every person will have a turn. Whenever you use this approach, it is good for you to go first. You can then model the depth of sharing as well as the appropriate length of time to take. It also gives everyone else a few minutes to reflect on the question (which you knew ahead of time). Your comments can give some perspective to the others in the group. Start with simple questions that everyone can respond to easily.

If someone seems to be dominating the conversation at any point, you can simply thank them for their comments and say you'd like to hear from another group member on that subject. Co-leaders of the group can do this very effectively, keeping the conversation of the group moving around its members. It is very important not to let one member run away with the group. Nothing will spoil the weekend more quickly for everyone else.

The best approach with someone who gets involved in telling long stories is to question them about what their real concern is. What made that time important to you? What did you learn from it? And then ask to hear from someone else on that point.

Most people do not realize how often they give unasked for

advice in response to someone's concern. It is a good thing for all of us to learn in a group. At one small-group overnight, it became a joke in the group, all of us laughing at ourselves and calling "foul" every time we did it. The funniest moment was when the leader accidently fell into the advice trap.

Intimacy is created as well by the focus for the weekend. We usually ask people to share around the circle during the first session on some question which is designed to help them get to know each other or to open up the level of intimacy. Several examples are:

1. "Share what you are looking forward to this weekend and what you are hoping to gain from your time here?"
2. "Tell something about you that is a gift you can contribute to the group during our time together and something you hope to receive from the group time."
3. "What part or parts of your life are going well right now? What are you feeling good about?"
4. "Think about the past day. What difficulties did you encounter trying to get here? What made it hard to get out?"
5. "What changes have happened in your life in the past year?"
6. "Describe briefly your spiritual background as a child."

A similar kind of question is good to use during the closing worship or communion before people leave. The question should help people share what they have experienced during the overnight and should help bring a sense of closure to the group.

Remember how special it is for people to have an opportunity to stand back from their daily lives, reflect on their spiritual journey, and take some new steps on that journey. Enable this by keeping the format simple and clear. Avoid crowding the schedule or setting more than one agenda for an overnight. Keep the environment one in which individuals feel safe and secure in their sharing and their reaching out.

It will be natural at the close of such an event for some of the participants to suggest that the group continue to meet. After all, nobody wants to come down from the mountaintop. Here, however, is a time to exert strong leadership. Unless the retreat was planned as a way of starting an ongoing sharing group, the group has to end with this retreat. People did not sign up with the agenda of continuing, and it is unfair pressure on some participants to have to continue meeting or to be left out if they cannot. It is healthy for the group to understand that experiences like this have beginnings and endings, and this retreat is now ending. If there are people who want an ongoing group to share some of the issues raised by the retreat, a new group should be convened at another time and place with the agenda of forming a continuing group.

Chapter 16
Sample Small-Group Overnights

T he following ideas are for different kinds of small-group overnights. They are arranged according to three categories: overnights for people with a common bond, spiritual retreats, and thematic overnights. Each of these types still fits within the procedures and framework described earlier in this section. Some of these retreats need only the facilitation of someone with good group skills. Others require a leader with specific training. Wherever possible, we suggest training and leadership resources.

Overnights for People with a Common Bond

The church is always balancing between affirming the unique individual gifts of its members and the common bond that all share in fellowship. Retreats are good ways to enable small groups of people with specific shared experiences to learn together. The most obvious groupings are men and women. To make a men's or women's retreat more specific, focus on men or women at major junctures in their lives, such as turning thirty, forty, fifty, or approaching retirement.

Women's retreats have special possibilities. Focusing on shared decades, such as turning thirty, forty, or fifty provides a special bond. Women who are parents of preschoolers, teenagers, or young people leaving home can enjoy sharing together. In gathering women with similar-aged children, it is important to keep the focus on the common concerns of the women rather than talking about the children. Single women, women recently divorced or widowed, can benefit from a retreat together.

In the same way men's retreats can offer unique opportunities unavailable to men anywhere else in society. Daniel Levinson's *Seasons in a Man's Life,* pointed out that men consistently report a lack of significant friendships developed after high school, the military, or college. Thus a retreat on male friendships is one possible theme. Shared decades, as described in the women's retreats, parenting, stress management, and health are all good themes for men. The following are some issues which both men and women can focus on on overnights:

1. friendships and relationships
2. balancing work and family
3. redefining goals and purpose
4. inner validations of the self
5. balance in your life: what is in balance? What is out of balance?
6. your support systems
7. balancing parenthood and/or marriage with your personal and professional goals.

Often a good novel or movie which deals with specific male or female issues may be the basis for an overnight if it is used to enhance the sharing of those who are in the group.

To keynote men's or women's retreats on issues such as these, it is necessary to formulate a few questions which will carry the theme through the weekend. For example, if the retreat is for men or women turning forty, the following questions would facilitate adequate discussion:

1. What were your expectations of yourself in your twenties?
2. What happened to those expectations in your thirties?
3. Where are the conflicts between your expectations and reality?
4. What are your expectations of yourself in the decade ahead?

Another common bond is being single. In the past five years, churches have become increasingly sensitive to the meaning of being single. Overnights for singles offer unique opportunities for sharing and growth impossible in the context of the larger church. Most denominations offer resources for singles. Contact the resource people available to you in your denomination or community prior to leading a single's retreat.

This is a place to realize the different needs of different size churches. In a small church, a singles retreat will need to include the concerns of newly widowed and divorced individuals, people who have been single for a long time, and people never married. The larger the church, the more possibilities there will be for overnights for any one of these groups.

The most important element in developing a single's retreat will be in communicating a positive approach. Here it is extremely important to recruit singles who are neither victimized by their status nor insensitive to the hurt of others. As key participants, they can help set the tone for the retreat.

Overnights are very special opportunities for married couples to explore the issues of their lives. The most highly developed program for married couples is the Marriage Encounter Movement, which has trained leaders throughout the country who are ready to facilitate weekend experiences. They can be contacted through your denominational offices. Marriage encounter emphasizes communication skills for healthy marriages. It recognizes that by the time many marriages get to counseling, it is too late. This early intervention model has been extremely helpful for many marriages.

It is also possible to run marriage overnights which are not full-fledged marriage encounters. Most marriage counselors are eager to work with church leaders in facilitating groups. As the church leader, you need to make sure that any outside facilitator understands the needs of your group. With or without that facilitator, it is important to keep the sharing simple.

One of the easiest and most rewarding marriage exercises is making a simple collage that represents one's marrige. Husband and wife cut out pictures from magazines separately, make their own collages and then take time to share them with each other. Another good means of sharing is to ask each partner to complete the sentence, ''It would be like Christmas for me if you would . . . .'' Each partner finishes the sentence and shares that which would bring them a Christmas-like joy. It seems obvious, but one of the hardest things for married partners to do is to be clear about their own needs. They expect their partners to be mind readers. After these Christmas wishes are shared, partners are asked to make the statement going the other direction, ''It would be like Christmas in our house if I did —— for you.'' This way marriage partners can see how well they communicated and were heard.

In a marriage weekend keep the questions positive. This is not a time for the unveiling of dark and dangerous secrets. Three elements must be present: time to think through their own joys and needs; time to communicate privately with each other; and time to share some of their thoughts and feelings with the larger group.

The typical pitfall is to overplan. Married couples don't often have opportunities to talk about their relationship with each other, so time fills up quickly. As with other groups, nurture participants and help them have a relaxing as well as challenging weekend.

These are not explicitly "religious" themes for overnights. Therefore, it is up to the retreat leader to include the spiritual questions and experiences in these retreats. Even though the themes deal with personal growth issues, there should be time for prayer and meditation. Resonating scriptures should be included. And there should be opportunity for worship, especially communion, on these themes. Other retreats, listed later, begin with the spiritual questions and move to the secular. Overnights for people with common bonds begin with the questions of daily life and then offer the spiritual underpinnings to those questions.

These overnights are different from classic retreats of men's or women's fellowships. Typically those are larger events, revolving around service projects or the expertise of invited speakers. These overnights are intended for small groups. They involve full participation of participants and rest on the belief that our shared brokenness is our strongest bond and that, in opening our lives to one another, God heals us.

Spiritual Retreats

For Catholics "retreat" means a quiet, reflective, spiritual experience. While much of the Protestant notion of retreat has developed into the variety of activities described throughout this book, the classic spiritual retreat has remained a mainstay in the life of the Catholic Church. It is being rediscovered in mainline Protestantism.

In the Catholic tradition, the retreat is run by a retreat master from a Diocesan retreat house. Any number of orders specialize in offering retreats. Retreats are offered throughout the year, and both clergy and laity participate. The retreat master selects a scripture for the retreat and reads it in the morning, giving comments and background for the session.

Retreatants then move into a time of silence and spend their time in prayer and reflection upon this scripture passage. The priest or retreat master schedules individual interviews with the participants to help them reflect upon the issues of their lives as they pertain to this passage. Books, commentaries, and articles relating to the passage are available for participants.

Later in the day, the leader offers further commentary on this passage. Evening worship is also centered on the passage. The emphasis is on time for silence, reflection, and spritual direction.

Protestants are welcome at these retreats. Contact your Diocesan headquarters for the names and descriptions of retreat houses nearby.

Protestant retreat centers are also beginning to offer retreats based on this model. For example, The Dayspring Church, a mission of the Church of the Savior in Washington, D.C., offers silent retreats at their farm in Maryland. The format is very similar to the Catholic retreat.

Variations within these traditions include stating a given theme for the retreat. Participants are also encouraged to explore their time of silence by exercising some of the right-brain skills such as drawing, poetry, or music. Pads of drawing paper, markers, charcoal drawing pencils are always available. Special music plays at different times in the main room. There is an emphasis on healthful food.

We had never participated in this kind of retreat until a few years ago. It was something very special for mainline Protestants such as ourselves who do not spend a great deal of time in silence. We hope that mainline Protestant leaders will take advantage of spiritual retreat opportunities offered at Catholic and Protestant centers throughout the country and bring these opportunities to their own congregations.

One model for offering a spiritual retreat is presented in packaged form by Rueben P. Job in a guidebook called *A Journey Toward Solitude and Community* (The Upper Room, Nashville, TN, 1982). A Leader's and Participants Guide present a retreat for spiritual formation in curriculum form. This particular program is something of a blend between the classic silent spiritual retreat and the traditional Protestant activity-oriented gathering.

To organize a spiritual retreat in your church, the first step would be to attend a few of these retreats yourself to get a sense of their meaning and direction. These quiet, gentle gatherings hold a promise for a new direction in spiritual renewal. But the resistance of highly verbal, task-oriented people will have to be overcome by bridging the gap between the study-oriented spiritual journeying most churches are accustomed to and the more intuitive quiet times offered to the soul in the classic spiritual retreat.

Thematic Retreats

Another way to organize retreats is on specific subject matter. It goes without saying that Bible study is always a good focus for a small-group retreat. In fact, a Bible study overnight may be just the bridge between the familiar retreats of most Protestant churches and the silent retreats of Catholic tradition. There are many Bible study approaches available through denominational curricula or independent resources. We mentioned the method used by Walter Wink in the Section II on Youth-Group Retreats. Wink's method of open-ended questions is described in his book *Transforming Bible Study* (Abingdon, 1980) and further amplified by Wayne Robinson in *The Transforming Power of the Bible* (Pilgrim Press, 1984). Each of these books lays out method and practical guides for Bible study on a variety of texts and themes. Their strength is that they combine the intellectual and intuitive gifts of the Spirit. They have the background of good solid scholarship that we were taught to respect in seminary, but have also opened the biblical texts again to exciting exploration. Opportunities for training in Bible Study with Walter Wink are available through Auburn Theological Seminary in N.Y.C., the Kirkridge Retreat Center, Bangor, PA, and through many other continuing education opportunities in places such as Iliff summer session, Denver, CO, and Union Theological Seminary, Richmond, VA. Any Bible study retreat should include time for silence, reflection, drawing, music, and meditation.

Another possibility for thematic retreats centers on growth therapies. There is often much to be learned from the means of communication and understanding in the psychological movements that catch the public eye. Co-leadership by clergy and a trusted therapist can produce exciting growing experiences when the issues of the spiritual journey are linked with the findings of Gestalt therapy, Jungian psychology, transactional analysis, psychosynthesis, structural family therapy, or popular discovery books such as Scott Peck's *The Road Less Travelled*. The clergy leader helps participants identify special moments in their spiritual journey through exercises such as a time-line describing the highs and lows of one's spiritual pilgrimage, or a collage that represents one's core beliefs, or even asking participants to think of their spiritual journey as a book and identify the title of the current chapter. A co-leader as therapist can then add other dynamic ways of understanding these same spiritual markers in life in ways which complement and enhance these moments rather than reduce them to some kind of analytic rationalization.

Making It Happen

Each kind of retreat, all-church, youth, and small-group adult, has its own kind of resistance which prevents it from happening. For the all-church retreat that resistance may be the difficulty of closing church for a Sunday. For the young people, it may be the dynamics of the family system. What keeps adult small-group retreats from happening? If we identify possible points of resistance, we can be that much more ready to enable these retreats to happen.

The first form of resistance is leadership. The most trusted leadership will typically be the clergy. If you are in a small- or middle-size church, it will obviously be difficult for clergy to take off many Sundays to lead adult retreats. There are three possible solutions here. The first is to hold overnights which begin on Friday and conclude by Saturday evening. This leaves the pastor free for Sunday services. The disadvantages are that this rushes participants from work to the retreat and tends to leave the pastor exhausted. The second solution is to arrange for the pastor to take off one to four Sundays a year to lead small-group retreats. The congregation may welcome this arrangement. The third possibility is to use resource persons from within and outside the congregation to lead retreats. This will mean careful training and trust building between these leaders and the congregation.

In a larger church, a staff member may be assigned retreat responsibility. It will be important to give that staff member enough time and authority to organize and schedule adult retreats.

The second point of resistance will be from members themselves. People are scared of new experiences, no matter how much they want them. Again there are three possible solutions. First, use existing groups as the core of these retreats. A Sunday school class, men's or women's group (if small), may be a place to start. The difficulty here is in including others outside the group and keeping the agenda off regular group issues. A second possibility is to do direct invitation and recruitment to people who have expressed general interest and whom you know would both benefit and contribute to such a weekend. Third, once you have tried solutions one and two, you now have a cadre of converts who may spread excitement enough for others to respond to general announcements. Post pictures of people having good experiences on those retreats. Help them share the positive meanings of these retreats without becoming overbearing.

A third source of resistance is the fear of being coerced to reveal more than one wishes in retreat settings. Memories of having been manipulated at church camps or pushed too far in encounter groups remain. The solution here is to begin by offering simple sharing groups in the church on the kinds of subjects which retreats might address. Build trust in these groups and then point out that retreats would be as safe and secure as these small groups.

Summary Reflections

On retreats, we encounter opportunities for spiritual growth, bonding with others of similar concerns, learning new paths, and envisioning new goals. These benefits are possible on retreats in ways which are totally different from such experiences in daily life. Thumbing through the gospels, you will notice that Jesus followed a regular cycle of engagement and withdrawal. His times of personal prayer and retreat were crucial to maintaining his spiritual center for his public ministry. His times of taking his disciples away with him to share with them were crucial to their learning. And the times he took just a few disciples aside were important to the vision they would need after his death and resurrection.

Without the journey inward that retreats enable, the journey outward soon burns us out. Small-group retreats, for bonding, spiritual growth, learning, and envisioning the future, are crucial elements in the rhythmic walk of faith. What is important for the spiritual development of young people and the community building of the whole church is equally essential to the spiritual care and nurture of the faithful adult.

Section IV

The Planning Retreat
by Jack M. Everitt

The Leadership Development Role of Retreats

Whether by intention or by accident, churches are often places where leaders are identified, trained, and developed through service on official or ad hoc boards. I suspect many civic, political, and business leaders could, if questioned carefully, trace their early development of management and leadership skills to serving as Sunday school officers, teaching youth and adult classes, serving on program, policy, or finance boards, or leading a church group through a problem-solving or planning session. The adult planning retreat provides a very special leadership development arena in that participants are removed from the pressure-filled "accountability" situations of their workplace and placed in a more relaxed, trusting environment. By intention, the planning retreat should "grow" leaders to fill increasingly responsible roles in the church. As for any other form of retreat, the planning retreat should provide opportunities for building individual confidence and self-esteem for each member of the group. The Reimers have provided excellent guidelines for planning, arranging, and conducting adult retreats of all kinds. This chapter will not repeat those guidelines, but will rather discuss the unique features of a planning retreat and will offer suggestions for success.

Business or Pleasure?

The planning retreat *should* contain intensive periods of "business."

Clearly, the overall goals of a planning retreat are *to plan, to solve a problem, to envision the future, or to develop an approach to an issue.* One common pitfall (particularly suffered by the business community), is to fail to schedule time for recreation and renewal. By scheduling time too rigidly or by "grinding out" a plan with few long breaks for walking, friendly conversation, or quiet reflection, we ignore all the research which clearly indicates that breakthroughs in thinking, planning, and problem-solving occur more often during "PQT" (Personal Quiet Time) than "in session."

The Why, Who, and How

Why do we conduct planning retreats for church members? Can't we make our plans for the year on a weeknight or Sunday after church? Shouldn't the minister and staff do the planning? Isn't the planning process simply giving people your recommendations and asking people to vote on them? Let's explore each of these questions to prepare ourselves for the "nuts and bolts" of getting on with the planning retreat.

1. Why do we conduct planning retreats?

Our lives as adults are filled with distractions. From car pools to corporate reorganizations, we all experience a great amount of "mind clutter" in our daily lives. The planning retreat provides a "protected" opportunity for small groups of adults to concentrate on a common purpose or issue. Again, breakthroughs in thinking are made more often in a quiet woodland, at the seashore, or on hiking trails than in weekly staff meetings or monthly church finance committee meetings.

2. Shouldn't the minister and staff do the planning?

The minister, in addition to his or her role as spiritual leader, oversees the business of a church much like the CEO (Chief Executive Officer) of a corporation. In any organization numbering more than a few members, the CEO cannot be directly involved in every aspect of the enterprise without suffering over-extension, fatigue, and eventual burnout. By delegating many business and program functions to lay members, the minister can focus on the "big picture," spiritual leadership, and other duties which uniquely belong in the ordained minister's calling.

3. Isn't the planning process simply giving people your recommendations and asking people to vote on them?

Sadly, this is a common method of planning. Many lay persons who chair church committees feel the need to "lead" by independently generating directives, goals, ideas, and recommendations which are then circulated to his or her committee for discussion and a vote. My advice here is to heed the words of a Chinese writer who said "when the greatest leader's work is done, the people say 'we did it ourselves.' " The earlier that committee members are involved in the planning process, the greater their eventual commitment to both the process and results. They become "stakeholders" and develop an early sense of ownership and in its "products."

In addition, by unilaterally handing down recommendations to be voted upon, the chairperson ignores the leadership development function of committee membership. By assigning leadership responsibilities to each member of the committee—whether "at home," or on retreat—the chairperson sends strong signals that leader development is an ongoing agenda item, and that leadership is a process to be shared by each group member.

The Who: Choosing Retreat Leaders

Perhaps you assume that the committee chairperson is the natural choice for retreat leader. In reality, the chairperson may not be the best choice. For planning retreats, an "outsider" is often the best choice.

Why Use an "Outsider" as a Leader?

It is difficult, if not impossible, for the chairperson to serve as retreat leader and effective group member. Several confusing signals are sent to group members when the chairperson serves as leader.

1. Are the chairperson's suggestions "the law," or merely input?
2. Is the chairperson processing the results in a nonbiased manner, or will the results be editorialized?
3. Is the chairperson's input being restricted by his or her duties as records, conflict resolver, or agenda manager?

The most appropriate role for the chairperson is as an equal participant in the process. Accepting this, how do you go about choosing a retreat leader?

The Traits of An Effective Planning Retreat Leader

Leading a planning retreat is a difficult assignment requiring well developed skills in two major areas:

1. Managing tasks.
2. Managing relationships.

Each area of leadership can be assessed by posing the following questions.

Managing Tasks

1. Has the potential leader demonstated an ability to move groups through an agenda without serious "sidetracks"?
2. Does the potential leader understand the basics of goal setting and action planning?
3. Does the potential leader possess a repertoire of group activities that serve to move the group along?

Managing Relationships

1. Has the potential leader demonstrated the ability to open the retreat with activities which set a tone of warmth, co-operation, and sense of group ownership?
2. Does the potential leader understand the role of social style (how each person communicates with others, such as domineering, sociable, standoffish, or skeptical) in involving each member to the fullest?
3. Can the potential leader spot trouble brewing between members and gently intervene to ward off personal afronts?

4. Has the potential leader demonstrated the ability to keep a group "on task" while allowing all members to express themselves?

5. Does the potential leader know how to close a retreat by summarizing, assigning follow-up tasks, and ending with positive affirmations and/or prayer?

A retreat leader who can provide a balance of task and relationship skills is ideal. The leader who is purely a "task master" will certainly carry out the agenda, but may intimidate group members, antagonize others, and exclude those who are less assertive. In contrast, the high-relationship "socializer" as leader may allow the group to lapse into a gossip session, personal therapy, or may end up deferring leadership to an aggressive task-oriented group member.

To locate an effective retreat leader, search your membership for those experienced in group process. Teachers, counselors, consultants, trainers, and recreation professionals often serve well in retreat leader roles. One major pitfall to avoid is selecting a leader purely for his or her power, prestige, position, or as a reward for faithful service to the church. To select such a person may, indeed, force them into an extremely uncomfortable role and end in failure for the retreat itself.

The Who: Attendees

This step in the retreat planning process often goes unattended. We assume that members of the particular committee involved plus a leader constitute a full planning group. The key question to ask when deciding who to invite is: who can represent the groups "back home" that will be affected by the results of the retreat? Using a church finance committee as an example, the retreat may be intended to evaluate past and future expenditures for all education and outreach programs and to recommend funding levels for the next three years. In addition to the finance committee, members of the various adult and school age Sunday school boards, pre-school board, home and hospital visitation committee, prison outreach, hunger project, family and marriage counseling board, the education minister, and business manager should be included. Each congregation will have a different set of constituencies. The above list is intended as a typical example.

By including the appropriate constituencies, you reinforce the stakeholders concept discussed earlier, and may diffuse potential resistance to your retreat's recommendations upon returning home.

The How: Preparing for the Planning Retreat

Once the retreat leader is chosen, he or she should meet with the group's chairperson and with the appropriate church staff members. Together, they make up the retreat planning team.

The specific steps for inviting people, getting them to the site, working out the costs and logistics, are covered by the Reimers in Section III.

The How: Special Techniques for Planning Retreats

Reread Section III for suggestions on developing a schedule and establishing trust.

As you move into the retreat itself, several planning and problem-solving techniques will be useful in leading you toward your goals. These techniques will be particularly helpful if you were unable to locate an outside leader, or choose to lead the retreat yourself.

When in Doubt: Brainstorm!

Done properly, brainstorming can get the retreat rolling, revitalize a "dying" retreat, or set the stage for a smooth closing. The rules of brainstorming are:

Ask a question, then allow each group member to respond *without judgment or criticism* from other members.
Example: After an opening icebreaker and introductions, ask the group, "For each of you, what can happen in the next day and one half that would prompt you to rate the retreat a "success"? Typical responses may be:
—Set expenditure levels and priorities for next year.
—Have a good time and relax.

—Decide about all these requests from non-church community groups for money.

List each response on newspirnt or chalkboard until you are satisfied that everyone has had an opportunity to contribute one or more expectations.

At this point you can post the list "as is" and refer to it during the course of the retreat, or you may wish to narrow the list to a smaller number of high-priority items.

Setting Priorities

With any list of "wants" or issues, a common pitfall is the myth of "everything is equally important." A list of concerns or issues for which there are no priorities is an invitation to intergroup conflict, misguided efforts, and diverted energy. I suggest the following method of setting priorities among a list of many items. Use the S.U.G. system.

For each item, ask each group member to assign a level of SERIOUSNESS, URGENCY, and GROWTH.

You may want to ask for these in writing in ballot form so as to reduce the "group think" produced by the assertive members of the group. For each item, each member determines whether or not the seriousness, urgency, and growth are H (high), M (moderate), or L (low).

Seriousness is measured in terms of the overall consequences of failing to deal with an issue.

Urgency is a measure of how soon you must deal with an issue before it adversely affects the church in some way.

Growth is a measure of whether or not the issue is getting bigger or worse, or whether it is static or is diminishing in its impact on the church.

Each item on the list must be rated for seriousness, urgency, and growth.

After everyone has rated each item, the leader tallies the ratings on the newsprint. Here's an example of a completed tally. (See p. 144).

Assume that eleven members rated each item.

By examining the array of ratings, it is clear that "set priorities for spending" is the #1 concern. "Hire a CPA" is #2. No other item has generated high enough ratings to merit time and attention *at the retreat.* However, this may be a good time for the chairperson

	H	M	L
S	‖‖/ //	////	
U	‖‖/ ///	///	
G	‖‖/	‖‖/	/

Set priorities for spending church funds on community projects.

	H	M	L
S		/	‖‖/ ‖‖/
U		///	‖‖/ ///
G	//	‖‖/ //	//

Answer criticisms of new purchasing procedure.

	H	M	L
S		‖‖/ ‖‖/	/
U		///	‖‖/ ///
G		‖‖/	‖‖/ /

Assign a task force to examine possible building expansion.

	H	M	L
S	‖‖/	‖‖/	/
U	////	‖‖/ //	
G	///	‖‖/ ///	

Determine criteria for selecting a CPA to review bookkeeping.

	H	M	L
S		/	‖‖/ ‖‖/
U	/	‖‖/	‖‖/
G		‖‖/	‖‖/ /

Make suggestions to youth group on how to raise money.

to assign the less serious, urgent, and growing issues to specific committee members for action back home.

Now the group can settle down to the tasks of:

1. Setting priorities for spending church dollars on community projects.
2. Determining criteria for selecting a CPA.

Before moving on, the leader should give members a final opportunity to express their concerns about lesser-rated issues. Many people feel that a "parting shot" is necessary before they can move on with the group.

Converting "Wants" into Goals, Objectives, and Action Steps

Each "want" or issue may need one or more *goals* to insure its achievement. Again, we are at a critical point at which many retreats fail. Here are two techniques that increase your chances of setting successful goals.

Stating Goals in the Present Tense

When beginning the goal-setting process, state goals *as if they have been achieved.* Let's take our issue of setting priorities for spending church dollars on community programs as an example.

Goal

The Church of XYZ *is* supporting worthy community programs through a set of guidelines which insure allocation of church funds to those programs which: (1) have a high impact on the disadvantaged population, and (2) have the highest need for our financial support.

By stating goals in the present tense, you create positive visions of the future. You can now set objectives which *lead up* to the goal being achieved.

Using SMART* Objectives

The letters S-M-A-R-T will help you to write effective objectives:

S = specific
M = measurable
A = attainable
R = relevant
T = trackable

If your objectives meet all the SMART requirements, you dramatically increase the likelihood of your goal being achieved.

Here's a SMART objective to support our previously stated goal of spending church dollars on community programs.

Objective One

To develop a "Request for Financial Support" form which asks community programs for information on their current activities, sources of funding, specific activity to be funded by Church XYZ, the benefits to the community of the activity, and the amount requested.

This form will be distributed to all community service organizations by June 30.

How did we do?

Is it Specific? Yes. A *form* will be developed.

It is Measurable? Yes. We can measure whether or not the listed items are included.

Is it Attainable? Yes. Many agencies, industries, and churches already have such a form. We can use them as models.

Is it Relevant? Yes. It will help us achieve our goal.

Is it Trackable? Yes. We have a June 30 deadline.

Now, the Hard Part

Once again we reach a point in the retreat where failure is possible.

(*From Kenneth Blanchard, Patricia Zigarmi, Drea Zigarmi, *Leadership and the One Minute Manager.* New York: Morrow, 1985.)

Often we set goals, write beautiful objectives, heave a sigh of relief and adjourn for volleyball or pack up to return home. *Who* is going to design the form? *How* will they get it done? *When* will they get it done? *How* will it be distributed? I urge you to complete the planning process by formulating *action steps* to fit each objective. The charts on pages 148-149 are an example of a "full process" plan for achieving one objective on the way to meeting our goal.

One Last Step to Strengthen the Action Plan

One exercise that I use with groups which appears to increase the retreat's likelihood of success is to brainstorm the *roadblocks* and *enablers* for getting the action plan accomplished. First, ask the group "when we get home, who or what might get in the way of our action plan's success?" List these, then ask "when we get back home, who or what can help us to carry out our plan?" List these, then ask "How can we reduce the roadblocks and get the enablers involved?"

Finally, spend a few moments discussing this question: "How will we communicate what we've done here at our retreat to the congregation?" People will want to know how you spent your time and energies. While I am not suggesting you formulate "group answers" to the congregation's inquiries, your general agreement on your accomplishments will serve to instill confidence by the congregation in your committee.

Objective One

To develop a "Request for Financial Support" form which asks community programs for information on their current activities, sources of funding, specific activity to be funded by Church XYZ, the benefits to the community of the activity and the amount requested.

This form will be distributed to all community service organizations by June 30.

Action Plan

Action Step	Who	When	Resources/Red Flags
Finance committee brainstorms items to	John Smith	May 12	Bring examples of forms from other organizations
Draft form for committee review	Jane Jones	May 24	Jane may need clerical help from church
Circulate draft to committee via mail	Jane Jones	May 30	Does Jane have current addresses?
Draft reviewed at next finance committee meeting	Jane Jones	June 15	Be sure to put it on agenda

Objective One (Continued)

Final typing	Joe Brown	June 19	John Smith will proofread
Master copy sent to church secretary	Joe Brown	June 21	Hand carry it
Church secretary sends to Community Service	Rita Doe	June 30	John Smith call Rita on 6/30
Call sample of organizations to make sure form arrived	John Smith	July 6	July 4th—holiday may delay

Why Planning Retreats Succeed:
A Checklist

1. *Good preplanning.* The chairperson prepares a careful checklist, convenes the planning committee and delegates key tasks to committee members. Planning should begin 180 to 90 days prior to the retreat date.

2. *The right people attend.* Choose representatives of those groups in the church which may be affected by your plans *and* from those groups which provide resources, decision-making authority or support for the results of your retreat.

3. *Attention to personal needs.* Choose a site, menus, and recreational facilities that will provide opportunities for everyone to relax.

4. *Good leaders.* A good process facilitator can steer the group through the stormy seas of disagreement and divergent perspectives.

5. *Clear goals and objectives.* Have the planning committee and the minister agreed on hoped-for outcomes? Why, exactly, are you asking ten busy people to spend 48 hours away from their businesses and families?

6. *Pace and flow.* Pay attention to adult attention spans. Schedule several short breaks instead of one long one. Use icebreakers to get the group going. Summarize often. Post an agenda and check progress frequently. Begin on time and end on time.

7. *Strong close with specific commitments.* Thank people for their work. Ask for feedback from the group about their feelings related to the retreat's usefulness. Review the action plan and confirm assignments.

Healthy, happy congregations don't just happen by accident or divine intention. Good planning, retreats of all kinds, and the intentional development of church leaders all lead to nurturing and maintaining what the Reimers call "The rhythmic walk of faith."

Appendix

Icebreaker Activities

S everal entry games are included below. They serve several valuable functions: they help people to relax; they help people to get to know each other; they mix up the group so that the same people are not together; and they set an atmosphere of fun and laughter. Entry activities can be used together at the beginning of the retreat, for perhaps 30 to 45 minutes. It is also possible to use one or two at the beginning of each adult session, depending on the nature of your adult program.

There are many resources for these activities, including:
Fun and Games by Rice, Rydberg, and Yaconelli (Zondervan Publishing House, 1977).
Prime Time for Families by Michael Pappas (Winston Press, 1980).
Serendipity Series by Lyman Coleman (Creative Resources, 1968-1974).

People Scavenger Hunt*

For each of the categories listed below, find someone with that characteristic. Have that person sign his or her name in the blank. When you have found someone for each item, sit down.
1) Someone who was born in 1950: _____
2) Someone who has freckles on his/her nose _____
3) The person with the longest (# of letters) last name _____
4) Someone who is not wearing socks _____
5) Someone with green eyes _____

6) Someone who was born in July _____
7) Someone who has been inside the cockpit of an airplane ____
8) Someone who has eaten frogs' legs and liked them _____
9) Someone who has been to Russia _____
10) Someone who doesn't know your last name _____
11) Someone who uses the same brand of toothpaste as you ____
12) Someone who can play the drums _____
13) Someone who speaks German _____
14) Someone over six feet tall _____
15) Someone who has a comb in his/her pocket _____
16) Someone who has hit a homerun _____
17) The person born closest to Christmas Day _____
18) Someone who does not like his/her middle name _____
19) Someone who can whistle "America the Beautiful" _____
20) Someone who dreams in color _____

*Note: This list is a sample of ideas. It is very effective to have some-
one design this list after a number of people have registered
for the event. Then specific items can be picked for people who
will be attending.

Do You Love Your Neighbor?

This game works best as the last game in a series of warm-up
activities, after people have been laughing and moving around.

Make a large circle of chairs, with one less chair than the
number of people. Everyone sits on a chair except for one person
who is in the center of the circle. That person walks up to anyone
who is sitting and asks "Do you love your neighbor?"

If the seated person says yes, then everyone in the room must
change chairs, moving at least three chairs away. The person who
is left without a chair is then in the center.

If the seated person says no, the person in the center then says,
"Well, who do you love?"

The seated person thinks of a category or characteristic and
says "I love everyone with red hair."

The people with red hair are then safe and remain seated.
Everyone else who does not have red hair has to change seats.

The game continues with new persons in the center for at least
ten minutes. There are all sorts of categories:

People with pierced ears
People with white socks
People who drank tea for breakfast
People wearing contact lenses
  Adults have a wonderful time playing this game as it has the strong nostalgia of childhood connected with it as you race to change seats.

Geography

Have everyone standing in a large room facing the same way. The leader has them imagine that the room is a replica of the United States, pointing out where Maine, Florida, California, and Alaska are. Then s/he asks the people to:
1) Go and stand where you were born. Greet the people who were born near you; share your stories of your birth.
2) Go and stand where you were living when you were twenty years old. Greet the people near you and tell each other what you were doing at that point in your life.
3) Go and stand where you went on your longest (farthest) vacation. Share stories of this vacation with the people near you.

*Note: Again, this list is a sample of ideas. Three sets of people moving and sharing stories is probably enough. You can substitute all sorts of ideas depending on the group:
  —stand where you had your first job.
  —stand where you went to high school.
  —stand where you lived when you were first married.
  —stand where you lived before you moved to your present location.

Name Tags

Name tags can be used for more than just names. They are opportunities for people to learn a little more about themselves and others. If you are looking for ways for people to build trust and share common themes in their lives, develop name tags which can focus on this information. Here are some sample formats:

A Name Tag Focusing on This Retreat

A word or two that
describes an early
retreat experience.

Two things you want
to have happen on
this retreat.

NAME

A word or two describing the biggest change in your life in
the past year.

A Collage Name Tag on Stages in Life

Use pictures from magazines which represent the following:

What you were like
as a child?

What you are like
now?

NAME

What you hope to be like
ten years from now.

A Self-Inventory Name Tag

Something fun you really
want to do this year.

What you are looking
for on this retreat.

Something you would do
with a $10,000 windfall.

If you could do
anything you wished
with your life, what
would it be?

Your NAME and four adjectives
which describe you.

A Spiritual Inventory Name Tag

The first Bible verse
that comes to mind.

NAME

My faith could be
summarized by the
sentence:

I am looking for
spiritual growth on
this retreat in
these three areas—
a.
b.
c.